African Mythology

STUART A. KALLEN

LUCENT BOOKS

A part of Gale, Cengage Learning

GALE
CENGAGE Learning·

Farmington Hills, Mich • San Francisco • New York • Waterville, Maine
Meriden, Conn • Mason, Ohio • Chicago

© 2015 Gale, Cengage Learning

WCN:01-100-101

LIBRARY OF CONGRESS CATALOGING-IN-PUBLICATION DATA

Kallen, Stuart A., 1955- author.
  African mythology / by Stuart A. Kallen.
    pages cm. -- (Mythology and culture worldwide)
  Includes bibliographical references and index.
  ISBN 978-1-4205-1145-1 (hardcover)
  1. Mythology, African--Juvenile literature. 2. Africa, Sub-Saharan--Religion--Juvenile literature. I. Title. II. Series: Mythology and culture worldwide.
  BL2462.5.K35 2015
  299.6'113--dc23
                                                    2014032490

Lucent Books
27500 Drake Rd.
Farmington Hills, MI 48331

ISBN-13: 978-1-4205-1145-1
ISBN-10: 1-4205-1145-9

Printed in the United States of America
1 2 3 4 5 6 7 19 18 17 16 15

TABLE OF CONTENTS

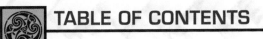

Map of the African Civilization

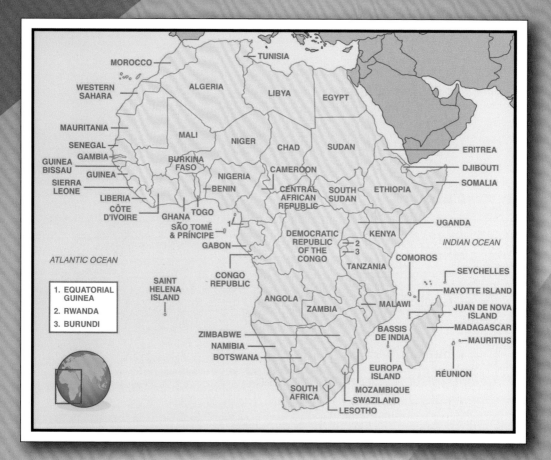

MOROCCO
TUNISIA
WESTERN SAHARA
ALGERIA
LIBYA
EGYPT
MAURITANIA
MALI
NIGER
CHAD
SUDAN
ERITREA
SENEGAL
GAMBIA
BURKINA FASO
DJIBOUTI
GUINEA BISSAU
GUINEA
CAMEROON
SOMALIA
SIERRA LEONE
NIGERIA
BENIN
CENTRAL AFRICAN REPUBLIC
SOUTH SUDAN
ETHIOPIA
LIBERIA
CÔTE D'IVOIRE
GHANA
TOGO
SÃO TOMÉ & PRÍNCIPE
1
UGANDA
GABON
DEMOCRATIC REPUBLIC OF THE CONGO
KENYA
2
3
INDIAN OCEAN
ATLANTIC OCEAN
CONGO REPUBLIC
TANZANIA
COMOROS
SAINT HELENA ISLAND
SEYCHELLES
MAYOTTE ISLAND
1. EQUATORIAL GUINEA
2. RWANDA
3. BURUNDI
ANGOLA
ZAMBIA
MALAWI
JUAN DE NOVA ISLAND
MADAGASCAR
MAURITIUS
ZIMBABWE
BASSIS DE INDIA
NAMIBIA
BOTSWANA
EUROPA ISLAND
RÉUNION
SOUTH AFRICA
MOZAMBIQUE
SWAZILAND
LESOTHO

Family Tree of African Deities

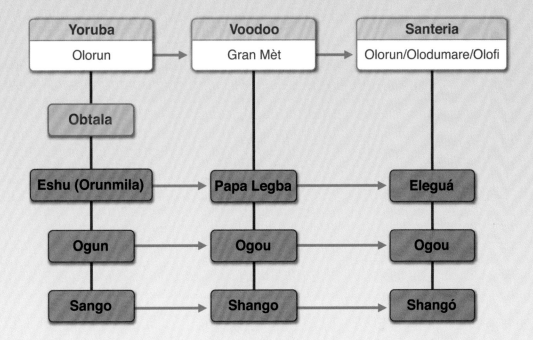

Major Entities in African Mythology

Name of Entity	Pronunciation	Description
Amma	AH-ma	The supreme deity of the Dogon people of Burkina Faso and Mali; the creator of the universe and everything in it.
Anansi	eh-NAN-si	A spider trickster of West Africa and the Caribbean; considered the god of knowledge.
Apedemak	ah-pa-DEM-ak	A lion-headed warrior god; the supreme deity of the Meroë people of Sudan.
Eshu	A-shew	Also known as Orunmila; the Yoruba trickster deity who acts as an intermediary between Olorun and humanity, with power over divination and sacrifices to other gods.
Ghede	GEED	The Haitian voodoo god of death, fertility, and the cemetery, said to be the corpse of the first man who ever lived. Ghede dresses in a top hat and smokes cheap cigars.
Legba	LEG-bah	Known as Elegba in Africa and Eleguá in Cuba, Legba is central to voodoo and Santeria rituals and is said to open the gate between the gods and humans.
Mebege	Meh-BEE-gee	The Fang deity who used a cosmic egg to create the world.
Obatala	o-bah-TALE-ah	The Yoruba god of humans, who were brought to life by the breath of the supreme god Olorun.
Ochún	O-choon	The Santeria orisha of the rivers, fresh water, and gold who reigns over love, female intimacy, beauty, and wealth.
Ogun	OH-gun	The second-ranking Yoruba god of iron, knives, the forge, and war.
Olorun	oh-loh-ROON	Also called Olodumare, the supreme Yoruba god, ruler of the sky and father of other Yoruban deities.
Orisanla	O-ri-SAN-la	The assistant who helped Olorun create all other gods and humanity.
Shangó	SHANG-o	Also called Changó or Xangô, the Santeria orisha of thunder, lightning, drums, and fire; among the most popular and venerated deities, perhaps because of his association with drinking and womanizing.
Yemayá	ye-ma-YA	The Yoruba spirit of the oceans, motherhood, and the protector of children, brought to the New World by slaves and incorporated into the Santeria pantheon.

The Way of the Ancestors

Africa is the second-largest continent on earth, making up about one-fifth of the earth's surface area. Africa is so big that it could hold the landmasses of the continental United States, China, India, and Europe and still have room for Argentina and New Zealand.

Africa is also humanity's first home; modern humans—or *Homo sapiens*—first appeared in Ethiopia around 160,000 years ago, according to fossil remains of skulls and bone fragments discovered there. As the world's first inhabited continent, Africa is also home to humanity's earliest mythologies. Around thirty thousand years ago, people known as the San painted mythological pictures on cave walls and cliffs in southern Africa. The art depicted creatures that appear to be part human and part animal. The human-animals are thought to be shamans, or spiritual healers who appear to be performing magical ceremonies based on myths and legends lost to time.

Healing, Dreams, and Visions

By around 2000 B.C. almost every region of Africa was populated by people who had their own mythology concerning the creation of the universe, life, death, spirits, deities, and magic. These tales were told in approximately eight hundred different languages and dialects. Yet according to African religious history professor Elizabeth Isichei, "African languages have no word for religion. Often the closest synonym was something like 'the way of the ancestors.'"[1]

Ancient Africans did not need a word for *religion* since spirituality was an important part of everyday life. Religious beliefs permeated African cultures from the Sahara Desert in the north to the continent's most southerly point, Cape Agulhas, South Africa. Across this 5,000-mile (8,047km) distance, people viewed society as a unity of visible and invisible worlds. The physical world, where people were born, lived, and died, was melded with the world of mythological ancestors, deities, and souls of children yet unborn. Additionally, as Isichei writes, ancient religious beliefs put an emphasis on "spiritual paths to physical and mental healing, and on dreams and visions."[2]

"God Made All Things"

With more than ten thousand tribal cultures, Africans cultivated an intricate range of mythologies that varied from place to place. However, most share a common belief in a universal, single god who created everything. This creator put humanity in Africa—which Africans considered the center of the world. This guiding principle of African mythology was summed up by King Lobengula of the Ndebele tribe of Zimbabwe in the 1870s. According to African history professor Ngwabi Bhebe, "[King Lobengula] said he believed in God and believed God made all things as He wanted them. He had made all the people, and He had made every country and tribe just as He wished them to remain . . . and it was wrong for anyone to seek to alter them."[3]

Africans believed that the universal god dwelled not on earth but in the heavenly part of the universe, home to the stars, sun, moon, and phenomena like lightning and the wind. God did not live alone; the heavens teamed with a population of messengers, servants, ministers, and childlike spirits.

While the supreme deity dwelled beyond the clouds, many African mythologies also described a powerful god-

In the 1870s Ndebele king Lobengula (shown) summed up African mythology by saying he believed in God and that God had made all things as He wanted them.

dess of earth. Mother Earth was described as the ruler of spirits representing rains, earthquakes, and other worldly phenomena. Many other earthly things—including mountains, waterfalls, rocks, forests, trees, insects, and animals—contained their own spirits, who were held in great esteem.

Wisdom of the Spirits

The concept of visible and invisible worlds extended to humans; each person was said to combine a visible physical body and an invisible soul. When people died, their soul entered the world of the spirits, where it could influence the lives of family members or even entire clans and tribes. Ancestors might appear during ceremonies or speak to the living in dreams. As photojournalists Carol Beckwith and Angela Fischer explain, "Ancestral spirits embody universal wisdom and are considered superior entities who live in close proximity to the creator god and can intercede on behalf of the family members they left behind. Custodians of tribal law and morality, these ancestors have the power to punish and reward and to maintain a society's equilibrium."[4]

The influence of ancestral spirits could be positive or negative. Some were viewed as personal guardians who protected communities from calamity. However, spirits not properly honored could mete out swift and stern punishment, which might include bad luck, sickness, and death.

Voodoo and Santeria

Traditional African mythology was practiced for thousands of years, but its development was interrupted when European slave traders began plundering Africa's population in 1502. In the 350 years that followed, an estimated 20 million Africans were kidnapped and forced into slavery. Millions died during the Middle Passage, the term given to the brutal voyage across the Atlantic Ocean from Africa to the New World.

Those who survived the Middle Passage brought ancient mythologies with them to the New World. These beliefs were blended with Catholicism, a religion imposed on the Africans by the slavers. The religions that evolved from this mix are called syncretic; they synthesize or combine two belief systems into a unique doctrine. The syncretic religions include voodoo (or vodou in Haiti), Santeria in Cuba and Trinidad, and Candomblé in Brazil.

Mythology in the Twenty-First Century

With 1.3 billion people, modern-day Africa is dominated by the world's major religions; about 90 percent of Africans are Christian or Muslim. However, many of these people also incorporate syncretic beliefs based on ancient African mythology. For example, many people attempt to heal their bodies, improve their luck, or remove curses by hiring shamans who perform ceremonies to communicate with spirits. There is also a widespread fear of witchcraft in parts of central and West Africa based on ancient mythologies concerning black magic and evil spirits.

An estimated 10 percent of Africans continue to practice the indigenous religions, or the ways of their ancestors. This number translates to about 130 million people who still believe the ancient mythologies that emerged along with humanity in central Africa. For these people, traditional African beliefs remain as important and relevant in the twenty-first century as they did to their ancestors five thousand years ago. As professor of African languages and literature Harold Scheub writes, "African mythology is a brilliant fusion of lavish imagination and austere belief, a flowing and unbroken intermingling of richly detailed, endlessly embroidered images moving majestically across the fertile terrain of this infinitely creative continent, a tapestry of images that poetically reveals deeply held faiths."[5]

Myths, Cultures, and Kingdoms

The mythologies of Africa are as old as the human race and are inhabited by gods, invisible ancestors, and all manner of natural and supernatural spirits. Each mythic being is associated with its own legends, deeds, and heroic journeys. Countless fabled figures have been forgotten over the ages while some remain widely recognized today.

The myths that have survived have done so because of an oral tradition; what is known today about traditional African mythology has been passed from generation to generation through the spoken word. The tales have been handed down by shamans, singers, musicians, dancers, and artists. The sagas of the gods and spirits were represented in folktales, songs, paintings, sculptures, and sacred shrines. And the mythologies laid the religious and cultural foundations for incredibly diverse tribes, clans, and kingdoms throughout sub-Saharan Africa, the vast region south of the Sahara Desert.

Links to Ancient Egypt

The cosmic mythologies of sub-Saharan Africa have elements similar to those of the ancient Egyptians. Beginning around 3200 B.C. the Egyptians built an advanced civilization along the banks of the Nile River; this civilization reached its peak around 1550 B.C. Anthropologists speculate that Egyptian mythology evolved from older sub-Saharan African oral traditions. Whatever the exact origins of Egyptian beliefs, they are well known today because they were recorded in hieroglyphs, a writing system based on pictures and symbols. Carved into buildings, stone slabs, coffins, and sheets of papyrus paper over thousands of years, the hieroglyphs describe the cosmic worldview that permeated ancient Egyptian society.

The Egyptians divided the world into three realms; the underworld, home to departed souls, the middle world inhabited by living beings, and the upper world of gods and goddesses. Although the Egyptians worshipped hundreds of deities, they believed that an all-powerful god, Amun-Ra, created all. As the ancient song "Hymn to Amun-Ra" states, "[You are] the Lord of Truth, father of the gods, maker of men, creator of all animals, Lord of things that are, creator of the staff of life."[6]

A Lion-Headed Warrior

Belief in the underworld, heavens, and an all-powerful creator god can be found in the mythology of the Meroë people. Around the third century B.C., the Meroitic Kingdom was established along the southern Nile in Nubia, near present-day Khartoum in Sudan.

The Meroë people mixed Egyptian mythology with their own ancient regional gods. Premier among them was a lion-headed warrior dressed in armor called Apedemak. Little is known about Apedemak, but the god seemed to hold warlike powers over men and beasts. Carvings of Apedemak on stone panels called reliefs show him standing, seated on a throne, or riding an elephant. He is also shown grasping prisoners of war and leading elephants and lions on leashes. Several magnificent temples were built to honor Apedemak by the rulers of Meroë around the first century B.C. In one the god is shown as a three-headed lion with four arms.

The Lion Temple of the god Apedemak in Sudan. The Meroë mixed Egyptian mythology with their own regional gods.

Archaeologists in the region have found ancient iron-producing blast furnaces and piles of iron waste called slag heaps. Apedemak was depicted dressed in metal armor to honor the importance of iron in Meroë's history.

Ogun and Iron

Iron also played an important role in other ancient African mythologies. After the Meroitic Kingdom collapsed in the first century A.D., the main center of African iron production moved west to Yorubaland. This region in present-day Nigeria, Benin, and Togo was, and remains, home to the Yoruba people.

Iron production, or smelting, was so important that the second-ranking Yoruba god Ogun was closely associated with the process. It was said that Ogun gave the gift of iron to the Yoruba along with the knowledge of smelting and the forge (iron furnace).

According to Yoruba mythology, Ogun originated as an unknown god. He became much more significant after he presented iron to heavenly spirits called orishas which surrounded the supreme Yoruba god Olorun when he created all things. (In the Yoruba language *Olorun* means "king of heaven" or "king over all.")

As the story of Ogun is told, some orishas wanted to live on earth but found that they could not maneuver in the dense forests. They tried to cut down the trees, but their only tools were made from wood, stone, and soft metal. Ogun arrived with an iron machete and used the long, razor-sharp knife to slice down the trees. The amazed orishas asked Ogun how he made such a strong blade. Ogun replied it was a secret.

The orishas begged Ogun to share the iron-making process, and he built a forge and made an iron spear, a knife, and other weapons for himself. But Ogun refused to share iron

Ogun was a patron of soldiers who wielded knives, arrows, and spears, as well as of hunters who used these weapons. A bronze plaque from the palace of the Obas of Benin depicts part of a war ritual in honor of the god Ogun.

with the orishas. Finally, the heavenly spirits struck a deal with Ogun. They would make him their ruler in exchange for iron. Ogun considered carefully and agreed. Afterward, Ogun went throughout Yorubaland to show both orishas and humans how to make iron.

Creator and Destroyer

Ogun was a patron of soldiers who wielded knives, arrows, and spears, as well as of hunters who used these implements to bring down big game animals. Ogun was also important to farmers, craft workers, and boat builders who relied on iron hoes, axes, machetes, and various carving and cutting tools. But the knowledge Ogun imparted to humanity could be used to create or destroy. It was said a good machete could clear a path to wealth, health, and prosperity; but if people neglected Ogun, they would be punished by slashing accidents, warfare, or other forms of bad luck.

As both a creator and destroyer, Ogun was portrayed with two images, according to anthropology professors Sandra T. Barnes and Paula Girshick Ben-Amos: "The one is a terrifying specter: a violent warrior, fully armed and laden with frightening charms and medicines to kill his foes. The other is society's ideal male: a leader known for his . . . prowess, who nurtures, protects, and relentlessly pursues truth, equity, and justice."[7]

The Yoruba offered prayers and sacrifices to benefit from Ogun's good traits and avoid the bad. A sacrifice might be a simple prayer. However, slaughtered animals like goats and chickens were seen as more precious since they served as foods to the gods. People also wore iron ornaments to draw on Ogun's power. These consisted of miniature charms, which hunters and warriors attached to clothing or hung from iron necklaces and bracelets.

Smelting Centers

Charms, along with arrows, machetes, sculptures, and other iron implements, were created by blacksmiths. These laborers worked with a very hard, iron-infused clay called *egun*. It was heated at high temperatures in an oven called a forge or

Smelting, Smithing, and Spirits

The lives of iron smelters, blacksmiths, and soldiers who relied on iron weapons were closely intertwined with the god of iron, Ogun. Anthropology professors Sandra T. Barnes and Paula Girshick Ben-Amos explain Ogun's significance to ironworkers:

Where ever they settled, ironworkers acquired significant ritual status. Their forges and smelters were seen as ritual shrines or sanctuaries for anyone losing a fight or fleeing turbulence. The anvil was widely used for taking oaths and as a sacrificial altar. Moreover, iron-workers (and hunters) organized into guilds, which served as [religious] groups organized around the worship of Ogun. . . . Smelting and smithing were separate occupations, plied by separate professional groups. Yet both groups in Yoruba-speaking communities looked to Ogun as their patron deity and both sacrificed to him. Iron-smelters who dug for their own ore, made sacrifices in order to find iron ore, to keep [mine] shafts from collapsing on them, and to prevent accidents while smelting.

Sandra T. Barnes and Paula Girshick Ben-Amos. *Africa's Ogun, Old World and New.* Bloomington: Indiana University Press, 1997, p. 52.

African ironworkers were organized around the worship of the god Ogun.

smelting furnace, which produced a type of raw iron called a bloom. Forges were located in iron-smelting centers located far from villages. This was done to protect villagers from dangerous flammable sparks and fumes produced by the process.

After the iron blooms were produced, they were transported to village blacksmith shops—every community had at least four. The blooms were reheated, hammered, and expertly shaped into valuable tools and artistic sculptures.

Because of their skills, iron smelters and blacksmiths were seen as sorcerers. It was believed that the ironworkers were endowed with divine or magical powers that allowed them to create something new by harnessing fire and elements of the earth. Anywhere iron was produced or fabricated was considered a shrine, as Nigerian-born historian Stephen Adebanji Akintoye explains:

> The iron-smelting center was a shrine of this deity, with all the adornment and paraphernalia of the shrine, and nobody who was not an initiate was allowed to come near it. The blacksmith's workshop was located closer to the village [than iron-smelting centers] and sometimes inside the village, and the villagers could come there to buy or repair their tools. But it, too, was a shrine and, like the smelting center, was a place of frequent sacrifices to the patron god Ogun. Even people who only used iron tools in their daily occupations (farmers, hunters, wood workers, sculptors, and so on) were supposed to offer sacrifices to Ogun. So highly did the Yoruba people esteem iron as a factor in their lives.[8]

Upper and Lower Realms

In addition to Ogun, the Yoruba believed in hundreds of lesser deities and spiritual beings who existed in a higher heavenly realm called *orun*. This world of spirits was divided into an upper sphere and a lower one. The higher world was home to the supreme god Olorun (also known as Olodumare). Olorun is associated with peace, harmony, justice, and purity, but he was so far beyond human understanding that people could not worship him directly. Consequently, there were few shrines to Olorun because the Yoruba were unsure which sacrifices to make to the supreme being.

The second heavenly sphere was closer to the world of humans and more easily understood. This realm was home to all other gods and spirits, arranged from the highest to the lowest in order of importance. The highest level contained orishas. The most senior orisha was Orisanla, who existed before humanity and all other gods and goddesses. It was said that Orisanla lived in empty space with his slave Atunda. One day while Orisanla was working in his garden, Atunda became rebellious and rolled a massive boulder down the hill. The boulder hit Orisanla and smashed him into hundreds of pieces, which grew into all the other orishas of the Yoruba pantheon. Orisanla grew whole again and assisted Olorun when he created the human race. Orisanla then married Odudu, a goddess viewed as the mother of all the gods.

Foretelling the Future

Because Olorun was beyond the reach of humanity, he used the powerful Eshu, god of chance, accident, and unpredictability, to act as a cosmic messenger. Eshu brought sacrifices to the god from earth and relayed Olorun's commandments to his human subjects.

While acting as a go-between, Eshu demanded a portion of the sacrifice for himself. If this was not done, Eshu would ensure the sacrifice had no effect and instead caused confusion and trouble. Because of this, Eshu was viewed as a trickster, a god who played tricks on humans. As trickster, he refused to follow normal conventions and started quarrels among friends, and impelled good people to commit evil deeds. The mythology of Eshu plays a major role in Ifa, the Yoruba system of divination, or the art of foretelling or seeing future events.

The divination system is named after Ifa, the Yoruba deity of wisdom. Still practiced today, the Ifa divination

Divination Worldwide

The ancient Ifa system of divination remains popular today in Africa and is practiced in the Americas by devotees of voodoo and Santeria. Believers can even download an Ifa app that allows users to perform divinations on smartphones and tablets.

ritual is a complex process that can be practiced several ways. One system requires sixteen nuts of the oil palm tree. A questioner tosses the sixteen palm nuts onto a sacred tray. There are 256 different patterns the nuts can make when they fall. The patterns are interpreted by a Yoruba diviner called a *babalow,* or father of secrets.

Each of the 256 patterns is associated with a chapter, or *odu,* in an immense volume of traditions known as *Odu Ifa.* Each odu contains 600 to 800 poems, which means the *Odu Ifa* contains as many as 204,800 poems. The shortest poem is four lines, and longer poems may be thirty pages. Each poem predicts future events, and most feature stories of individuals, deities, and spirits. Akintoye describes the *Odu Ifa*: "In its final form, the *Odu Ifa* became the longest corpus [body] of poetry in Yoruba folklore, a massive and ever-growing cultic body of wisdom encompassing historical and mytho-

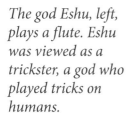

The god Eshu, left, plays a flute. Eshu was viewed as a trickster, a god who played tricks on humans.

logical accounts, exalted precepts [teachings], snippets of divine wisdom, life-related instructions, and the profoundest of the Yoruba philosophy."[9]

Clients never state their problems to the *babalow*. The clients are left to interpret the poem as it relates to their personal problem or question. Once the divination is finished, it is time to satisfy Eshu. The *babalow* instructs the client to make specific sacrifices at an Eshu shrine set up outside the diviner's door. Eshu then takes the message of sacrifice to the appropriate spirits involved with the predictions. The offerings are necessary either to ensure that forecasts of good fortune come true or to prevent disasters that have been foretold.

The Herbalist

In addition to sacrifices, some verses of the *Odu Ifa* call for the client to purchase magical herbal powders or potions. The concoctions are prepared by an herbalist called an *onisegun* who specializes in divination, magic charms, and the supernatural.

Herbs might be used for good purposes—attracting love, success, and wealth—or evil purposes such as causing an enemy to suffer. Herbal mixtures have supernatural purposes such as making a client invisible, providing visions in dreams, or enhancing the power to read minds. As folklorist and anthropologist William Bascom writes, "[Herbal] medicines are compounded to protect against witches, avoid death, keep out thieves, kill one's enemies, cause them to go mad, or simply make continual trouble at home for them."[10]

The herb preparations of the *onisegun* might be put in a client's drink or food. They can be rubbed on the body or placed under small cuts made in the skin. Herbs are burned, sprinkled around an enemy's door, or brushed on a spear or machete for luck. The mixtures can also be packed into magical amulets that are worn around the neck, wrists, or ankles.

Herbalists sell expensive concoctions with rare ingredients to kings, chiefs, and warriors and simple powders to poor farmers and hunters. Because of their perceived power, *onisegun* are both feared and respected.

The Knowledge Seekers of Ife

Between the eleventh and sixteenth centuries, the city of Ife in present-day southwestern Nigeria was a spiritual center for the Yoruba people. Nigerian-born historian Stephen Adebanji Akintoye explains:

Many groups sprang up in the era of Ife's economic, political, and cultural primacy, each seeking to advance its own brand of knowledge: knowledge of herbs, of the past (or history or mythology), of the invisible forces at work in the world, of divination, of the making of magically effectual articles (or charms), of the hidden "secret" meanings and power of words, of hidden (occult) names for ordinary objects, of out-of-body projections, of access to the power of witchcraft for "wisdom" and other beneficial purposes. . . . Ife was the home of the greatest concentration of cultic [religious] knowledge and power. Traveling in order to know more and to teach was a common preoccupation of the cultic groups. . . . Ife became the place to which the "wise" came from all over Yorubaland and beyond to acquire some special knowledge—and to add to the stock of special knowledge.

Stephen Adebanji Akintoye. *A History of the Yoruba People.* Dakar, Senegal: Amalion, 2010, p. 74.

Ife: The City of Heaven

According to Yoruba mythology, the Ifa divination system arose and was perfected in the city of Ife in southwestern Nigeria. Sometimes called Ile Ife, the city was a thriving center of Yoruba civilization in the eleventh century. Like many other aspects of the culture, Ife was viewed through the lens of myth and mythology. The Yoruba believed that Ife was the place of all creation. It was the source of life and the place where human enlightenment rose like the sun in the sky. Ife was so close to heaven people expected to meet their deceased relatives walking its streets. It was said the gods had their homes in Ife and the gate to heaven was at a shrine hidden somewhere within the city.

Whatever its relation to heaven was, Ife was also an earthly delight. As the most powerful and prosperous city in Yorubaland, Ife was filled with beautiful adobe buildings featuring carved wooden posts and doors. The walls of open-air courtyards were decorated with colorful mosaics, murals made from small tiles.

Ife residents created beautiful, intricate sculptures from bronze, iron, copper, and red clay called terra-cotta. Sculptures of human figures—effigies of kings—had important mythological meaning. When a king died, the sculptures were buried under a shrine dedicated to the ruler. When annual rituals were held to honor the king, the sculptures were unearthed for ceremonies and then reburied.

From around 1000 to 1500, Ife was home to the most famous and respected people in Yorubaland. Some were so revered and powerful that their names replaced those originally given to ancient deities. For example, the ancient god of lightning and thunder, Jakuta, was renamed Sango after a Yoruba king. Eshu came to be called Orunmila, after a great Ife *babalow* who traveled all over Yorubaland practicing and teaching Ifa divination. Orunmila also made his mark on the *Odu Ifa*, which mentions his name numerous times.

Ife residents created beautiful, intricate sculptures from bronze, iron, copper, and baked red clay called terra-cotta. This thirteenth-century terra-cotta sculpture depicts a sacrificial victim.

Bantu Hero Epics

Even as Ife was growing into an important religious, cultural, and economic center in West Africa, another civilization was settling in central and southern Africa. The Bantu people consist of around five hundred different ethnic groups. They speak closely related Bantu languages and dialects that represent the largest language family in Africa. Around 1500 B.C. the Bantu homeland was located along the border of eastern Nigeria and Cameroon. Over the course of many centuries, Bantu people migrated to central, southern, and southeastern Africa, where they either displaced or absorbed indigenous cultures.

By 500 B.C. Bantu-speaking communities were established in the rain forests of central Africa and the grassy savannahs in the present-day Democratic Republic of the Congo, Angola, and Zambia. Other Bantu people moved to East Africa and present-day South Africa. The migration continued until about A.D. 1000, when the Bantu occupied more than one-third of Africa. Wherever the Bantu settled they brought their language, culture, farming methods, iron-production technology, and mythology.

Like the Yoruba, the Bantu developed a complex mythology based on ideas concerning an all-powerful god and numerous spirits including those of ancestors who meddled extensively in daily affairs. Bantu mythology is intertwined in hundreds of epic sagas, long tales recounting the deeds of heroes who undertake mythical quests. Bantu heroes journey to distant lands, the underworld, or the sky, where they might suffer terrible ordeals. Many stories contain monsters such as gnomes said to possess a single deadly, blood-red, razor-sharp tooth. Another Bantu monster is the half man with one eye, one arm, and one leg; the other half of his body is made of wax.

The most fearsome type of Bantu creature is the evil ogre, a swallowing monster that devours humans, villages, and even entire countries. The Bantu-speaking Sotho people of South Africa

The Owl of Death

In Bantu mythology hearing the hoot of an owl by one's front door was a sure sign that a family member would soon die. The misfortune could be prevented by chasing the owl away with a flaming stick.

A nineteenth-century engraving depicts a Bantu warrior. By 500 B.C., Bantu-speaking communities were established in the rain forests of central Africa and the grassy savannahs in present-day Democratic Republic of Congo, Angola, and Zambia.

tell of an ogre named Karnmapa, who passed from village to village swallowing people, dogs, chickens, goats, and cows. Karnmapa was killed by a baby-hero who turned into a grown man moments after birth. The hero cut up Karnmapa and freed the creatures in its belly. Like most Bantu sagas, this one ended with the hero returning home in victory and receiving rewards such as many cattle and a kingship.

Omens and Dreams

The heroes in Bantu sagas looked for assistance from omens and dreams. In this way the heroes were like everyday Bantu people who sought to foretell the future by random events such as the weather, the behavior of animals, and even bodily processes.

The Bantu people seek omens about a child's future as soon as it is born. Birthmarks on the skin can have negative or positive consequences. For example, the Abaluhyia people of Kenya believe that a child born with a mysterious scar is gifted with special qualities that will help him become a rainmaker, doctor, chief, or diviner. Babies who cry all the time, teethe early, or use their left hand are said to exhibit negative signs. These traits are said to foretell a future in which the child grows up to be a troublemaker or a criminal. Families of such children apply herbal medicines and perform rituals to reverse the influence of these ill-fated behaviors. Odd physical afflictions in adults are also seen as omens of evil. A sudden twitching in the eye, a loud unexplained noise in the ear, or repeated sneezing means something nasty is about to happen.

Like people of many other cultures, the Bantu assign great importance to dreams, which are viewed as a link between the spiritual and physical worlds. The meaning of some dreams can be obvious; nightmares are seen as omens from evil spirits, and dreams about prosperity are a sign of impending good fortune. Other dream interpretations might be harder to understand. For example, seeing or eating roasted meat in a dream is a sure sign of imminent death, especially if the meat is impaled on a stick. However, such dreams are welcomed by the chronically sick, who can then see the peacefulness of death near at hand.

Whatever the meaning of a person's dreams, the myths and legends of the Bantu strongly influenced hundreds of other cultures occupying the African continent. When added to the legends of the Yoruba, the mythologies covered a huge portion of sub-Saharan Africa and united people in belief systems as complex as any on earth. From the more than two hundred thousand poems of the *Odu Ifa* to fears of roast meat on a stick, the mythology of Africa has permeated cultures and kingdoms for thousands of years.

CHAPTER 2

Creation Myths

Nearly every culture in the world has a story that describes the creation of the world, all living things, and the sun, moon, and stars. Some of the oldest creation accounts come from sub-Saharan Africa, where the idea of one supreme creator is nearly universal.

Various African words describe the creator as the High-God, the Sky God, the Old One, and the First Ancestor. The creator is most often male and referred to as "father." Scholar and historian J.B. Danquah explains how his people, the Akan of Ghana, describe the supreme creator: "The father of the family, the father of the tribe, the race of man, and indeed all things, or as the phrase goes in Akanland, the Creator of the Thing, the universe of being."[11]

For the Yoruba, the supreme creator, Olorun, was more than the first father; he was the perfect emperor of the universe. According to Sierra Leonean theologian Harry Sawyerr, the Yoruba call Olorun "the Pure King, the King who is without blemish, and the King with unique and incomparable majesty who resides in heaven."[12]

The Palm Tree to Heaven

According to Yoruba legend, before Olorun created the world there was only sky above and water, swamps, and mist below.

One of the orishas who lived in the sky was named Obatala. One day Obatala asked Olorun for permission to create a solid world beneath the sky where the orishas could walk and live. Olorun granted permission, and Obatala went to the god of divination, Orunmila, for help. Orunmila peered into the future and suggested that Obatala make a golden chain to descend from the sky. He was told to climb down the chain carrying several items he could use to create the earth: a snail shell full of soil, a hen to spread the soil, a black cat to act as a companion, and a palm nut.

Orunmila directed Obatala to pour the soil on the water and place the hen on it. After this was done, the hen scratched the soil and spread it in all directions. Obatala planted the palm nut in the soil, and it instantly grew into a tree, creating many more nuts. The numerous nuts sprouted into palm trees wherever there was soil. Obatala told Olorun the earth needed more light, so the supreme god created the sun and the moon and sent fire to earth on a vulture's head.

A Bantu sacred grove honoring Osun and other deities at a shrine for the god Obatala.

Things were going well, but Obatala was lonely on earth with only a cat to keep him company. He shaped human

bodies out of clay and asked Olorun to breathe the life force into them. This force, called *ase* in Yoruba, was also given to earth spirits, animals, plants, rocks, and rivers. In addition, *ase* gave life to language. Words used in songs, prayers, praises, curses, and even daily conversations were given spiritual powers that could exert a good or bad influence. This meant speakers needed to be careful; negative statements, songs, or prayers might have serious consequences.

The People of Obatala

The Yoruba god Obatala created people with disabilities while drunk on palm wine. Today Yorubans with congenital defects are called *eni orisa*, or "people of Obatala." And those who worship Obatala are forbidden to drink palm wine.

There was a problem when Obatala was shaping humans from clay. He became thirsty and drank a great quantity of palm wine. In a drunken state, Obatala made many misshapen figures with twisted limbs, bent backs, and other problems. When he sobered up, Obatala vowed to be a protector of all people with disabilities.

The people Obatala created thrived and grew in number, but they needed food. To help them, Obatala gave humans the copper knife and the wooden hoe so they could grow grain and yams. As humanity prospered, Obatala saw that his work on earth was done. He climbed back up the golden chain and returned to the sky, where he continued to live with the orishas.

The Cosmic Egg

In some cultures the creation myth evolved around a single god who created the universe with what is called a cosmic egg. This egg was said to contain everything and provide the catalyst for all life. One cosmic egg story is traditionally told among the Fang people of equatorial Africa. In the beginning the supreme god Mebege sat alone in heaven above the empty primeval waters of the universe. A mythical spider called Dibobia hung below Mebege on a long strand of web. The spider asked the god to create the earth.

Mebege took a smooth pebble from the sea, material from his brain, and hair from under his right arm. The god blew a single breath over the material and created a cosmic egg. Dibobia lowered the egg into the sea. Mebege fertilized the egg, and three beings emerged: the male god Zame, his sister, Nyingwan, and his brother, Nlona.

Zame (sometimes spelled Nzame) took control of creation. Nyingwan helped, providing a drop of blood from her heart to deliver harmony and balance to earth. Nlona reached into his brain and added a white substance, a part of his mind that represented good and evil.

Zame created termites and worms. Dibobia poured the termites into the ocean, where they pulled the seabed up to the surface to form land. Zame went on to create almost everything else: earth, sun, moon, stars, animals, and plants.

Zame asked Mebege if he had done well. According to scholar of African mythology Clyde W. Ford, Mebege replied, "We see many animals, but we do not see their chief; we see many plants, but we do not see their master."[13] In response Zame appointed three kinds of animals as masters of all things. Elephants were picked for their wisdom, leopards for their cunning and power, and monkeys for their malice and agility.

Zame remained unsatisfied with animals as masters, so he created exact copies of himself and his sister. According to Ford, Zame told the copies, "Take the earth. You are henceforth the master of all that exists. Like us you have life, all things belong to you, you are the master."[14]

He Who Rests upon Nothing

The Dogon people who live in the mountainous regions of Mali also tell a cosmic egg story. The story begins with the Dogon creator god Amma, whose name means "he who rests upon nothing." Amma created the egg of the world, called Po, which means "seed" in the Dogon language. Po was an egg that contained the entire structure of the universe, but it was also the smallest thing in the world.

The world began when Po was shaken by seven huge rumblings that caused the egg to divide into two birth sacs, or placentas, each containing a set of twins fathered by Amma. The four were androgynous, with both male and female characteristics. Each of the four beings represented important aspects of Dogon mythology, but one set of twins, Ogo and Nommo, dominate the creation story.

Cloth Is the Center of the World

The Dogon of Mali believed that human language began with the first word, which was weaved into cloth by the deity Nommo. The word was used to build culture and civilization. Based on this mythology, Dogon weavers were viewed as sacred along with their tools, looms, and the cloth they produced. French professors of ethnology Marcel Griaule and Germaine Dieterlen discuss the importance of cloth to the Dogon:

The Dogon make a large range of narrow lengths of cloth, plain-colored and striped, the most usual colors being indigo, white, and red; these are used chiefly to make clothing and blankets. Weaving is held to be one of the original crafts, and innumerable symbolic images are associated with it. It is said that "cloth is the center of the world," that it expresses everything, since . . . all things were traced in it. The *Nommo* who invented weaving used his jaw-

bone for loom and his tongue for shuttle [a tool designed to carry thread to a loom]. He wove into the cloth the words which were bringing in a new order.

In another way the weaver imitates the *Nommo* who, springing from the clavicles of God, forthwith wove together the four elements contained therein and made from them the whole universe. Just as he drew the four elements from the clavicles of God, so the weaver draws his threads—that is, the four elements—from the spindles [of] the loom. . . . To wear a particular cloth, to possess a certain blanket, is therefore to display a symbol which . . . corresponds to the physical or moral condition of the wearer, to his social and religious functions and his ordinary activities, which are themselves in harmony with the rhythm of the universe.

Quoted in Daryll Forde, ed. *African Worlds.* London: Oxford University Press, 1968, pp. 106–107.

The Dogon of Mali believe human language began with the first word woven into cloth by the god Nommo. Dogon weavers were highly revered and their tools, looms, and cloth were deemed sacred.

Dogon cave paintings depict the Dogon creation myth and Amma Serou falling from heaven.

Problems began before the twins hatched. Ogo broke out of the egg and abandoned his twin. The solitary Ogo descended into the primordial darkness with a piece of the placenta, with which he created the earth. But Ogo was lonely, so he tried to climb back into heaven to rejoin Nommo. When this act failed, Ogo descended into the bowels of the earth. Ogo's piece of placenta soon rotted, bringing death to the earth.

Amma punished Ogo for his rebellious and disorderly acts by turning him into the Pale Fox, a creature that travels only at night. In Dogon mythology this made the fox the enemy of light, water, fertility, and civilization. However, the Dogon believed the fox had the power to reveal the future and hidden truths if his tracks in the sand were read properly.

Amma was unable to alleviate the disorder unleashed by the Pale Fox, so he sacrificed Nommo, a perfect being. Nommo's blood flowed through the universe and gave birth to the heavenly bodies, animals, and edible plants. Nommo's dismembered body purified the world's four cardinal points (north, south, east, and west). In this role Nommo came to represent order, fertility, and life.

Cries, Grunts, and Screams

Back in heaven, Amma continued his work. He created an ark filled with pure earth, made from Ogo's broken placenta. Amma brought Nommo's shattered body back to life and placed it in the ark with four new pairs of recently created twins. The ark was lowered to earth on a golden chain, and it dropped onto the land created by Ogo during the world's first rainstorm. which had created a pool of water. The sun rose for the first time, and Nommo went

A miniature of the god Nommo. Nommo is said to have spit out threads of cotton on which were contained the first words. Nommo used his jawbone for a loom and weaved the word-threads into cloth.

to live in the water. The eight twins became the ancestors to all humanity, cultivating fields and spreading through Ogo's impure world.

The first beings were unable to communicate well. They could only express themselves like infants, with cries, grunts, and screams. Nommo solved this problem from his place in the pool of water. He spit out threads of cotton that also contained the first words. Nommo used his jawbone for a loom and weaved the word-thread into cloth.

The words were heard by one of the eight original ancestors, who used his drum to echo language to the others. In this way the first words were entwined in a cloth with the first musical rhythm. Equipped with these new tools, the ancestors learned to weave, build houses, farm, sing, play music, and dance. Eventually, the ancestors invented marriage by exchanging sisters.

Symbolically, the Dogon creation story describes the various stages of life. It begins with conception, spirits in a helpless fetal state floating in the placenta or womb. The newborns emerge as a life force both chaotic and creative but mute. They learn speech and music, grow into adolescents, and become educated in the ways of the world. The first humans move into adulthood when they go to work, enter into matrimony, and create cloth and homes. All these changes take place on the earth nurtured by Ogo's decaying placenta, a symbol of death that eventually claims all.

"All Is Yo"

The belief in a sacred word that spurs creation is shared by the Bambara (or Bamana) people. The Bambara share Mali with the Dogon and also populate Guinea, Burkina Faso, and Senegal. They are part of the Mandé ethnic group, a large family of people who speak the Mandé language. The Mandé founded some of ancient Africa's most advanced empires, including the Mali and Songhai Kingdoms.

According to the Bambara, in the beginning at the primordial void of the universe there was a single sound: *Yo.* The vibration of that root sound was responsible for the for-

In the Beginning There Was *Yo!*

The word yo *was so popular among hip-hop performers in the late 1980s that it spawned a TV show called* Yo! MTV Raps. *The word* yo *is still used today to grab someone's attention in place of words like* you *or* hey. Yo *has also been used for thousands of years by the Bambara of Mali, who believe it was the first sound and assisted in the creation process. Clyde W. Ford, scholar of African mythology, ponders the modern and ancient uses of the word* yo:

A cacophony of sound during the day, city streets can recede into desolate silence at night. One evening I walked down such a street, devoid of people, traffic, and noise, without the comings and goings that infuse the city with life. Mesmerized by this pause in the urban pulse, I was suddenly shocked by a disembodied voice calling out loudly, "Yo," then again in escalating tones "Yo . . . yo." For a moment "Yo" hung in the air, resounding off sidewalks and building walls, looking for escape to the void from whence it came. I mused over the personal depths of this sound—a plaintive wail, shrill exhortation, a moment's recognition? I would never know. Smiling to myself, I continued on, knowing the ancestors would be pleased. Through whatever fate this monosyllable had found its way into popular urban slang, I was certain that few who uttered it knew that Yo was spiritually gifted. The Bambara of Mali believe the universe begins and ends in the sound of Yo. So along with its echo down that urban corridor, I also heard the sound of the origins of creation itself.

Clyde W. Ford. *The Hero with an African Face.* New York: Bantam, 2000, p. 170.

The African word yo *was said to have been the first sound uttered at Creation. Today it is known in America as a basic part of hip-hop vocabulary.*

mation of every single thing, including human awareness. As the Bambara tell it:

> In the beginning there was nothing but the emptiness of the void (fu). The entire universe began from a single point of sound, the root of the sound of creation, *Yo*. . . . Emanations from this void, through the root sound Yo, created the structure of the heavens, of the earth and of all living and nonliving things. Yo comes from itself, is known by itself, departs out of itself from the nothingness that is itself. All is Yo. Out of the void the vibrations of Yo gave rise to *gla gla zo*, the highest state of consciousness. Gla gla zo ultimately manifested itself in the creation of human consciousness.[15]

The Bambara creator figures Faro, Teliko, and Pemba were brought into being by Yo and went on to formulate various parts of the world. Faro was a female water spirit who created seven parts of the earth that reflected the beauty of the seven heavens. These were fertilized with rain. Teliko was the spirit of the air who created a set of twins who were the first ancestors of humanity.

Pemba created soil, then mixed dust with his saliva to create a woman named Musokoroni, whom he married. Pemba and his wife then went on to create all the animals and plants. However, according to legend, Musokoroni was jealous of Pemba's power, so she planted him like a seed in the ground. After doing so she wandered the earth alone, causing chaos and misery while spreading sickness and death. When she was about to die, Musokoroni atoned for her sins by teaching agriculture to humanity. Finally, Faro took over the job of spreading happiness and harmony on earth. She also dug up Pemba and freed him. It was said that Faro would return to earth every four hundred years to make sure everything was still in order.

The Tree of Life
The power of a sacred word provides a common basis for other African creation myths. The story told by the Wapang-

wa of Tanzania features a creator known as the Word. Before the existence of the sun, moon, and stars, the only things that existed were the wind and the Tree of Life, where white ants lived. There was also the Word, which controlled everything but could not be seen.

The Word became the catalyst for creation after the wind grew angry and blew a branch off the Tree of Life. The ants that lived on the branch were hungry after they fell to the ground. They ate all the leaves off the branch except one and used this last leaf as a place to defecate. With all the leaves gone, the ants had no choice but to eat their excrement, which piled up until it became a mountain. The pile eventually grew so large it approached the top of the Tree of Life. The ants now had more food to consume, and their waste pile swelled so large it formed the earth with its mountains and valleys.

One day after the world was formed, the Word sent a cold wind that formed white frost, or snow. This was followed by a warm wind that melted the snow and caused a huge flood that killed all the ants. Later the waters receded, and the Word joined with the Tree of Life to create trees, grasses, rivers, and oceans. The Word joined with the air to create animals, birds, and humans. Each had its own song or language.

Killing the Word

Earth's new animals were hungry and wanted to eat the Tree of Life. Humans defended the tree with sticks and stones, setting off a great war between people and animals. This led to the practice of humans and animals eating each other. The war became a huge conflagration that caused the earth to shake violently. Chunks of the earth flew into space. Some grew so hot as they hurled though space that they became the sun, moon, and stars.

Finally the war ended. This caused a long-tailed sheep with a single pointed horn to jump for joy. The sheep leaped so high that the sun set her on fire. In this way she became the source of thunder and lightning. But the sheep killed the Word. New gods sprang to life after the great war ended, but the deities were unhappy with humanity. According to the

Wapangwa, one of the gods, the brother of the Word, told humankind:

> You men kept a sheep, you made war, and your sheep became mad—it flew through the air and it killed the Word, from which all things that adorn the world have sprung. Well, I am the younger brother of the Word. And I tell you, you were great, but because of the things you have done, you shall be reduced, you shall be small until in the end your height shall not even be half of your present stature. And in the end your entire world will be consumed by fire.[16]

The belief in a sacred Word of creation is not confined to sub-Saharan Africa. The biblical book of John 1:1 in the New Testament states: "In the beginning was the Word, and the Word was with God, and the Word was God. . . . And the Word was made flesh and dwelt among us."[17] Similar theological ideas about the sacred word predated the New Testament and can be found in ancient Greek and Egyptian stories of creation. This concept is also found in the ancient Hindu texts known as the Upanishads, which describe a single, powerful word: *Om*. "This eternal Word is all; what was, what is, and what shall be, and what is beyond in eternity. All is Om."[18]

Life and Death

In addition to covering the creation of the universe, earth, and humanity, some African mythology explains how specific aspects of the world came into being. Of those aspects, none is more important than life and death, realities that are central to human existence. The Baganda of Uganda developed a complex account concerning the origins of life and death. The myth is called the "Story of Kintu."

Long ago there was only one person living on earth, Kintu, alone with his cow. Up in heaven the creator of all things, named Ggulu, had many children, including a beautiful daughter Nambi, who liked to come down to earth to play. One day Nambi met Kintu and fell in love at first sight.

In the beginning was the word, & the word was with God, & the Word was God.

John, ch.I.v. 1.

Pub. by Alex Hogg to C° Paternoster row.

begins: "In the beginning was the Word, and ... all things were made through [the Word]."

Nambi wanted to marry Kintu and move to earth. Ggulu did not approve of his daughter marrying an earth creature and demanded to meet Kintu. Nambi took Kintu to heaven, where Ggulu made him perform a series of difficult tasks. After Kintu successfully accomplished the tasks, Ggulu approved of the marriage and presented his daughter with wedding gifts to make a home on earth. Nambi was given

...ken and Millet

The Baganda goddess Nambi disobeyed her father and returned to heaven to retrieve millet seed to feed her chickens. In traditional Baganda society, wives are required to serve chicken to their husbands and male in-laws. This makes millet chicken feed an important possession for a married woman.

chickens, cows, goats, sheep, seeds of millet grain, and banana-like plantains.

Ggulu had one warning for Nambi; once she left for earth she could not return. If she did, her evil brother Walumbe, or Death, would accompany her back to earth, where death did not yet exist. However, after leaving on her journey, Nambi remembered she had left the millet behind. She needed the seeds to feed her chickens. Kintu warned her not to return to the sky, but Nambi ignored him. When Ggulu saw her, he said, "Didn't I tell you not to come back for anything that you forgot and that if you met Walumbe, he would not allow you to go with Kintu alone?"[19]

At that moment Walumbe appeared and complained that Kintu had taken his sister away and he wanted to accompany her back to earth. Ggulu agreed, but Nambi was upset. She said, "We are not going to be able to manage him because he is [insane]. How are we going to cope with Walumbe?"[20] Despite Nambi's protest, Walumbe went to earth.

Nambi went on to have three children with Kintu. After a time Walumbe asked his sister and Kintu for one of their children to work as his servant to cook and clean. Kintu refused to give one of his children to Walumbe. After Nambi and Kintu had more children, Walumbe returned to ask for another child to act as his servant. When Kintu again refused, Walumbe threatened to kill all his children. Kintu was confused because at that time death did not exist in the world. However, the children began to die.

Kintu complained to Ggulu but was reminded that Nambi had ignored the warning when she had been told not to return to heaven. Now the children were dying. As the tale continues, Nambi's other brother, Kayiikuuzi, enters the story. Ggulu said Kayiikuuzi would try to capture Walumbe and return him to heaven. However, Kayiikuuzi's efforts failed when Walumbe escaped into the underworld. Finally, Kintu gave up and said Walumbe could continue to kill his children. But, according to Kintu, Walumbe "will not be able to finish all of them because I, Kintu, will always continue to beget [produce] more."[21]

Adapting the Story

In some ways the Baganda creation story mirrors the tale of Adam and Eve in the book of Genesis in the Bible. In that story Adam and Eve were the first man and woman. They lived in paradise, the Garden of Eden, where peace and happiness were eternal. Like Ggulu warning Nambi not to return to heaven, God warned Eve not to eat the fruit from a tree in the garden. Just as Nambi returned to heaven, Eve disobeyed God's order. Because of this act, Adam and Eve were cast out

There are many similarities between the Old Testament story of Adam and Eve and the Baganda creation story.

of the Garden of Eden. They were forced to live in a world of suffering and death, just as Nambi and Kintu had to watch some of their children die. However, the children of Adam and Eve, like the children of Nambi and Kintu, went on to populate the earth.

The similarities between Nambi and Kintu and Adam and Eve were obvious to the Baganda people. According to religious studies professor Benjamin C. Ray, when Christian missionaries traveled to Uganda in the 1870s and told them the story of Adam and Eve, "the Baganda immediately recognized the similarities with their own story of creation, especially about the origins of marriage, death, children, and human suffering. . . . [Uganda] Christians began to adapt the story of Kintu and use it in Christian teachings."[22]

In this way the Baganda story, like many African creation myths, is universal. Composed in the far distant past and handed down through the generations for centuries, the myths provide basic answers about creation that are still addressed in the modern world.

CHAPTER 3

Animal Tricksters

Many African legends are solemn and deal with serious topics such as birth, death, and the troubles of the world. Other stories, distinguished by their humorous tone, involve animals such as rabbits, foxes, and spiders. These stories, called trickster myths, involve amoral and comical animals who use tricks and deceit to fool people into carrying out schemes that often fail or backfire. Sometimes the tricksters purposely plot to have a plan fail in order to benefit somehow from the disaster.

Tricksters often exhibit extreme examples of human behavior to manipulate their victims or survive. Tricksters can be greedy, stupid, lazy, cunning, destructive, excessive, and erratic. Sometimes the behavior is also contradictory; one minute a trickster is heroic, and the next it is an amoral villain.

Trickster tales are beloved because they entertain children and make people laugh. But they also pass along important moral lessons such as the consequences of bad behavior. Those harmed by tricksters' schemes, as well as tricksters themselves, often come away wiser after their difficult experiences.

The Spider Trickster

Tricksters can be human or supreme beings called divine tricksters. But most often they are animals that use their intelligence and cunning to triumph over larger creatures. The spider, which appears in dozens of African folktales, is a perfect example. With its power to spin thread and ensnare large prey in its web, the spider appears as the trickster Gizo in Niger and Nigeria, Ture in the Congo, and Wac in Sudan.

The most renowned spider trickster, Ananse (or Anansi), originated among the Ashanti people of Ghana and the Ivory Coast. Over the centuries, the Ashanti developed a large body of mythology about Ananse called *anansasem,* or spider stories. Although Ananse is a spider, he often acts like a man. Sometimes he wears clothes or has a human face. He might also appear as a human being but with eight spider legs.

Ananse originated as a rival to the supreme Ashanti god Nyame. After Nyame created the earth, Ananse created the sun, moon, stars, and rain. Ananse also added common virtues, vices, and afflictions that are often contradictory. Ananse provided disharmony and cooperation, sickness and health, wisdom and stupidity, and even the state of contradiction itself. The spider trickster also embodies opposing principles. Ananse is the deceiver and the deceived, the betrayer and the protector, the creator and the destroyer. Above all, Ananse is driven to outsmart others and create disorder.

Traditionally, storytellers begin Ananse tales by stating that the story is not true, though it often reveals basic truths about the human condition. These tales contain the wisdom of the Ashanti people and are meant to provide insight into the ups and downs of daily life.

Ananse Buys All Stories

The Ashanti believed Ananse was the god of all stories and knowledge. He came to own all stories that were ever told by purchasing them from Nyame. The price was very high, but Ananse had a good reason to want all stories because they contained all wisdom. If Ananse owned all legends, everyone in the world would have to seek his advice before they embarked on any new plan.

Ananse came to own all the stories after Nyame offered them in exchange for three things: the hornets, the great python, and the leopard. To capture the hornets, Ananse

The African Origins of Brer Rabbit

In 1879 the *Atlanta Journal-Constitution* published "The Story of Mr. Rabbit and Mr. Fox as Told by Uncle Remus," written by Joel Chandler Harris. The story was the first of many by Harris to feature a clever cottontail named Brer Rabbit. The stories were very similar to African trickster tales imported into the United States by West African slaves during the eighteenth and nineteenth centuries. Harris spent four years working on a southern plantation, where he heard the traditional stories told by slaves. He created the character Uncle Remus to narrate the Brer Rabbit stories. Uncle Remus is depicted as a kindly old former slave who speaks in a thick southern dialect.

The American Brer Rabbit tales are based upon similar African trickster tales.

Harris's Brer Rabbit books, including *Uncle Remus: His Songs and His Sayings*, were best sellers. But today the stereotype of Uncle Remus is viewed as demeaning to African Americans. Nonetheless, as English professor Trudier Harris writes, the tales often contained thinly veiled references to the hardships faced by slaves and their attempts to outsmart their white oppressors: "The violence and come-uppance that characterize these tales, frequently with larger animals (whites) being bested by the smaller Brer Rabbit (blacks) . . . [portrays] a world where the weak and the witty always triumph over the powerful and the presumed intellectually superior."

Trudier Harris. "The Trickster in African Literature." National Humanities Center, June 2010. http://national humanitiescenter.org/tserve/freedom/1865-1917/essays/trickster.htm.

cut a hole in a gourd and filled it with water. He climbed the tree where the hornets lived and poured water over them. Ananse insulted the hornets, saying they were foolish to stay in the rain. Then he offered to save them, using the gourd as a hornet shelter. The hornets flew into the gourd, and

Ananse plugged the hole. He gave the gourd full of hornets to Nyame and went on to his next task.

To capture the great python, Ananse cut a long bamboo pole. He visited the python and told a lie. Ananse said he was arguing with his wife about whether the python was longer or shorter than the pole. After some convincing, the python allowed Ananse to tie him to the bamboo to straighten him out for a proper measurement. Once the python was secured on the pole, Ananse delivered him to Nyame.

Finally, Ananse set out to capture the leopard. He dug a pit in the ground and covered it with branches and leaves. The leopard fell into the pit, and Ananse offered to rescue him. The trickster spider bent a tall tree down toward the ground and tied it place. He attached a rope to the top of the tree and dropped the other end into the pit. Ananse instructed the leopard to tie the rope to his tail. After this was done, Ananse cut the rope holding the bent tree. When it sprang upright, it left the leopard swinging in the air by his tail. In this helpless position, Ananse had no trouble tying up the leopard and taking him to Nyame. Once the final price was paid, all the stories in the world belonged to Ananse.

Collecting All Wisdom

Once Ananse owned all the stories, some people were ungrateful and resented the spider trickster's power over all wisdom. This displeased Ananse, so he decided to punish humanity by repossessing his wisdom. He went house to house with a giant gourd and collected the tidbits of knowledge he had handed out. He decided to store the gourd high atop a large tree where no one would find it.

Ananse tied the gourd across his chest and tried to climb the tree, but the heavy load prevented him from getting a good grip. After several unsuccessful attempts, Ananse's young son, Ntikuma, offered some advice. He told Ananse to hang the gourd from his back. This

Best-Selling Spider God

The best-selling 2005 fantasy novel *Anansi Boys* by Neil Gaiman is based on a character who is an incarnation of the West African spider god Ananse.

made Ananse angry. He said he must not have gathered all the wisdom in the world, since Ntikuma obviously still had some. However, the suggestion was a good one, and with the gourd tied across his back, Ananse was able to climb the tree.

When he reached the treetop Ananse was agitated. He said, "I might as well be dead. . . . I collected all the wisdom (or so I thought) in one place, yet some remained which even I did not perceive, and lo! my child, this still-suckling infant, has shown it to me."[23] This disturbed Ananse so much he hurled the gourd of knowledge onto the ground, where it smashed on a rock. People who saw this ran over and began grabbing bits of wisdom. The first ones to arrive picked up a great deal of wisdom. Those who came later were only able to grab bits and pieces of knowledge. The story concludes: "This is how everyone got wisdom; and anyone who did not go there in time (to pick some up) is—excuse my saying so—a fool."[24]

In this story Ananse is sufficiently generous to hand out wisdom, but selfish enough to take it all back. He is stupid when he tries to scale the tree with the gourd on his chest and petty when offered simple advice from his son. Finally, he creates disorder when he scatters wisdom but in doing so distributes knowledge to humanity, even while creating fools.

The Not-So-Clever Tortoise

Among the Yoruba the tortoise Ijapa is Ananse's counterpart. Like the trickster spider, Ijapa can be ambitious and lazy, arrogant and shy, wily and oblivious. Ijapa's main weakness is his boastfulness. Because he cannot keep his mouth shut, his enemies are often able to gain the upper hand. His strength is his singing voice, which he uses to cast spells on people and cause them to do his bidding. Like a modern cartoon character, Ijapa often dies but is brought back to life for other trickster tales.

In one tale in which the tortoise dies, Ijapa thinks he is being clever and cannot stop playing tricks until his scheme goes horribly awry. This story gave rise to the Yoruba proverb that states, "When Ijapa is doing something, he will not stop until disaster falls on him."[25]

The tale begins with Ijapa suffering from hunger. The tortoise is too lazy to grow his own food, so he wanders from farm to farm looking for food to steal. He finds a farm where the field is brimming with yams ripe for the digging. Ijapa is not satisfied to dig up just a few yams and foolishly tries to steal them all. But his load of yams is too heavy, and the struggling Ijapa is spotted by a farmer, who runs up to the tortoise brandishing a huge knife. The farmer swings and tries to chop off Ijapa's head, but the tortoise quickly pulls his head inside his hard shell.

The angry farmer picks up a big rock to smash Ijapa's shell, but the tortoise begins to sing. While weaving a beautiful melody, Ijapa tells the farmer the only way to kill him is to bury him under a large pile of grain. Under the spell of the tortoise's song, the farmer fetches a basket of millet, pours it over Ijapa, and covers him with a large pot. The next day the farmer returns expecting to find a dead tortoise, but after lifting the pot he sees Ijapa is fat and happy, having eaten all the grain.

Ijapa is so pleased with himself he sings another magical song to help him escape. At that moment a priest passes by on his way to a shrine honoring the medicine god Osanyin. Ijapa convinces the farmer to hand him over to the priest. The priest carries Ijapa to the shrine of Osanyin. However, the priest had been seeking items to sacrifice to the god, and tortoise meat was the perfect offering. Ijapa was killed and sacrificed, and the priest was rewarded with good fortune by Osanyin.

Clever Thieves

A second tale about the tortoise and the yams has a better ending for Ijapa. Once again the trickster tortoise is too

Tortoises carved on an African jewelry box testify to the importance of the myth of Ijapa.

lazy to tend a garden or store food for lean times. When a drought strikes, Ijapa and his wife, Yanrinbo, face starvation. After unsuccessfully begging for food from passersby, the couple decides to steal yams from a neighbor's storeroom. To conduct the theft, Ijapa stands upright. Yanrinbo climbs up the tortoise's back, sits on his shoulders, and places a basket on her head. They break into the storehouse and fill the basket with purloined yams.

When the neighbor discovers the theft, the tortoises do not appear so clever. The neighbor follows the footprints to Ijapa's house and seeks justice by bringing the tortoises before the chief. Ijapa and Yanrinbo claim they are innocent, so the chief puts them to a test. He gives them an herbal drink that will make them sick if they are lying but will not hurt them if they are telling the truth. The cunning Ijapa then states he never stretched up his hands to steal the yams. Yanrinbo says she did not use her legs to carry away the yams. Since Yanrinbo used her hands to steal the neighbor's yams while sitting on Ijapa's shoulders, they both are telling the truth and neither become ill. In this way the tortoises outsmarted the humans, even though they were obviously the thieves.

The Hare, the Hippo, and the Elephant

Tricksters often outsmart more powerful creatures, and the wily hare is no exception. Among the Bantu-speaking people of Angola, Botswana, and Namibia, the behavior of a hare named Kadimba often mirrors that of other trickster animals. In the tale of the hare, the hippopotamus, and the elephant, Kadimba is in the same predicament as Ijapa; hungry and too lazy to work.

Kadimba needs his field to be cleared so he can plant a crop, but he is unwilling to labor in the dirt. The hare decides to trick an elephant and a hippo into doing the work instead. To lay the groundwork for his scheme, Kadimba stretches a rope across the field and hides in some nearby bushes. When

The Tortoise and the Hare

"The Tortoise and the Hare" is an ancient Greek fable about a tortoise who is ridiculed by a hare. The tortoise challenges the hare to a race and wins by being clever and wily. This story, like many traditional fables, has its roots in ancient African trickster myths.

An Ogoni tribal mask of Kadimba, the hare trickster.

the elephant walks by, Kadimba makes a bet with the giant creature. The tiny hare bets the elephant cannot beat him at a tug-of-war. The laughing elephant agrees and picks up the rope with his trunk.

Kadimba then runs across the field and once again hides behind some bushes. When the hippopotamus comes along, the hare makes the same bet. The hippo is amused and picks up the other end of the rope in his teeth. Kadimba then jumps into the bushes and tugs on the rope. At this signal the elephant and hippo, who cannot see each other, begin pulling on the rope from opposite sides of the field. The stubborn animals refuse to stop. They continue to tug back and forth all day and all night. Finally, the puzzled elephant and hippo give up, each wondering how a hare could beat him.

Kadimba was very happy; every time the elephant and hippo pulled on the rope, they plowed another row in the hare's field. After the tug of war, Kadimba was able to plant his seed without doing much work.

Hare of Life and Death

In another tale, Kadimba was more helpful to people. It seemed there was a thief named Dikithi who stole cattle and ate all the meat without sharing. The desperate people had no food, so they begged Kadimba to come to their aid. Using

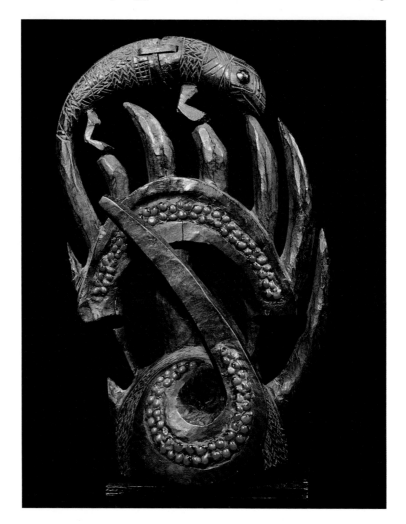

An African dance mask depicts the chameleon that the god Nyambe sent to earth to tell humans they were blessed with eternal life.

his trickster magic, the hare captured hundreds of fireflies. He placed these in Dikithi's clothing. When Dikithi went to steal more cattle, he thought the glowing fireflies were the eyes of Kadimba watching him. Fearful that Kadimba might capture him, Dikithi ran away, leaving sufficient food for the local villagers.

Instead of granting life, sometimes the hare plays the opposite role and acts as a messenger of death. Among the Luyi of Zambia, the supreme god Nyambe sent a chameleon to earth to tell humans they were blessed with eternal life. But the fleet-footed hare arrived first and told people that once they died, they would stay dead forever.

In a tale told by the Khoikhoi of South Africa, the hare makes a clerical error that results in the creation of death. In this tale the moon sends the hare to earth with a message. The hare is to tell people that the moon once died but is now reborn. As such, humans will also be reborn after they die. But the hare is confused and mistakenly inserts the word "not" in the message; it reads that because the moon died and was reborn, people would die and *not* be reborn. When the moon found out, it was so angry it hit the hare, splitting the hare's lip. This is why hares now have split upper lips.

The Ant Brings Bread

Not all animals portrayed in African mythology are devious tricksters. Some are said to help humanity survive. The tiny ant is one creature that plays a large role in African mythology. The Berber and Kabyle people of Mali, Niger, and Burkina Faso have a myth based on a wise ant who provides dietary instructions to the first man and woman, who lived underneath the earth.

One day the man and woman detected small piles of seeds and grains lying on the ground. They peered down and saw a tiny ant struggling to remove the husk from a single grain of wheat. After many hours passed, the ant was finally able to eat the grain. The woman was tired of watching the ant and wanted to step on it, but the man wished to continue his observations.

The man could not understand why the ant was working so hard for so little food. He asked the ant why he did not eat the grain with the husk still on it. The ant replied that the tenderest part of the grain was under the husk. The best way to prepare the grain was to cook it in the spring water found on the surface of the earth. The man and woman had never heard of water, so the ant offered to take them up to earth and show them a spring.

When the man and woman came to the spring, they tasted the water and were amazed by its freshness. Then they dropped grain in the water and tried to eat it, but the grain was hard and hurt their teeth. The ant laughed and showed them several large stones. The ant told the humans to grind the grain into flour. The man and woman followed the ant's instruction and tasted the flour. Once again they scowled at the taste. The amused ant said the grain still was not ready to eat. He showed them how to mix the flour with water in an empty gourd to make dough.

The man and woman tasted the dough but were still not impressed. The ant laughed again and showed them how to start a fire with dried grass, wood, and a flint stone to spark the material to flame. The ant told them to lay a flat stone in the ashes of the fire and lay the dough on top. As the dough baked, the man and woman began to wonder why they needed to work so hard when they could just eat berries and leaves. But once the hot cakes of bread were finished, the couple broke off pieces and ate them. It was so delicious they ate every last crumb.

In one final lesson, the ant showed the humans how to save barley and wheat seeds and sprout them in water. When the rainy season came, the man and woman planted the seeds and were able to harvest fields of grain to make bread.

The Serpent Da

Of all insects and animals that appear in African myth, the snake, or serpent, is perhaps one of the most powerful. Serpents are symbolic of health, fertility, rain, lightning, thunder, and the rainbow. Because serpents shed their skins, they are often symbolic of renewal, rebirth, or immortality. Among the Fon people of Benin, the serpent is called the Da and is seen as the driving force of life. As the Fon saying goes,

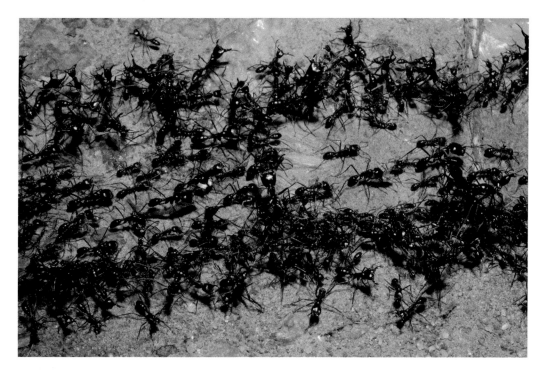

"All things which curve, move, and have no feet are Da. What makes my hand move, my head move? It is the Da in me."[26]

The lowly African ant plays a large role in African myth.

According to the Fon, the serpent once carried the supreme creator god Mawu in its mouth. As Da and Mawu created the world together, mountains grew from the snake's excrement. Precious minerals were contained in the mountains. The rising and falling hillsides followed the curved outline of Da's snake body. When he moved, the serpent created earthquakes.

The Fon traditionally believe in a second serpent, a female also referred to as Da, which exists in the sky. The female uses her tail to hurl thunderbolts down to earth, and her arched body makes the rainbows.

In Fon tradition, when babies are born into the world, Da is represented by the umbilical cord. The umbilical cord is then buried beneath a palm tree. As a symbol of Da, the cord helps plants grow life-giving roots. As the Fon say, "When we pull up a plant from the ground, there are roots. If we cut away the roots, the plant dies. The roots are life. They have the quality of Da, for they are flexible, living, and have no feet, and are moist."[27]

The Audacious Da

Traditionally, the Fon people of Benin hold the serpent Da in great esteem. The cosmic snake once had a devoted following of men who created religious shrines to Da. However, Da required proper worship or trouble might come to pass. Anthropologists Melville J. Herskovits and Frances S. Herskovits explain:

Only a man of property, one who has control of the wealth and wellbeing of a household may enshrine his Da . . . before his compound. . . . Two pots, both covered, one for the male and one for the female [serpent] constitute a shrine. This "establishing" of a [shrine] insures prosperity to the household over which he has control, for Da is the giver of prosperity. . . .

Da is a thief and a fickle one for what he gives to one he takes away from another. When enshrined and properly [appeased], he makes a slave of a weaker Da, that is, a Da whose owner has not properly cared for him—takes all from him and uses him as an emissary to rob other Da. This weaker enslaved Da is angry and evil; he is called Danglato—the audacious Da.

Melville J. Herskovits and Frances S. Herskovits. *An Outline of Dahomean Religious Belief.* Menasha, WI: American Anthropological Association, 1933, p. 57.

Da himself seeks nourishment from iron bars made by monkeys who live in the sea. It is believed that the world will end when the Da's iron food is gone. The hungry male serpent will devour his own tail, and the earth will fall into the sea. The Da serpent is not a trickster but is viewed as a guardian of sacred places, good luck for hunters, and ruler of various aspects of nature.

The Trickster in the Modern Age

Trickster stories have roots in ancient Africa, and they took on new life when brought to North America by African slaves. Stories of the trickster hare were told and retold over generations and evolved into what came to be known as the Brer Rabbit stories. Brer Rabbit, like the trickster Kadimba, featured a wily rabbit who used his wits to overcome challenges and exact revenge on those who tried to harm him.

Brer Rabbit was featured in extremely popular children's books in the early twentieth century and was the basis for the 1946 animated Disney feature *Song of the South*. The behavior of the cartoon character Bugs Bunny can also be traced to the mischievous deeds of the African trickster hare.

Tricksters also appeared in literature written by African Americans. The 1952 novel *Invisible Man*, by renowned author Ralph Ellison, addresses racism and other social issues faced by black Americans in an era when blacks were

African tales of a trickster rabbit appeared in America in stories of Brer Rabbit told by fictional former slave Uncle Remus. Shown are Remus and his young listener in the 1946 Disney film Song of the South.

expected to be submissive to whites at all times. One of the characters, the narrator's grandfather, explains the trickster traits he used to deal with white people: "Overcome 'em with yeses, undermine 'em with grins, agree 'em to death and destruction, let 'em swoller you till they vomit or bust wide open."[28]

In less serious stories, tricksters came alive in film and television. In *The Pirates of the Caribbean* film series (2003–2011), the notorious pirate Jack Sparrow achieves his goals using a trickster's wit, deceit, and pranks. In the long-running animated TV series *The Simpsons*, Bart Simpson is the ultimate trickster. Bart often ends up in trouble for his fake sincerity and devious deeds but always seems to learn a lesson in the end.

Since ancient times African storytellers have understood that good parables benefit from mischievous characters who exhibit the best and worst of humanity. Whether listeners are laughing or shaking their heads in disbelief, a memorable story needs unforgettable characters, some of whom live on for centuries.

CHAPTER 4

Spirits, Magic, and Ceremonies

The term *animism* is central to African mythology. Animism is defined as the belief that nearly everything—including animals, plants, rocks, lightning, and the dead—possesses vibrant spirits. The spirits are nearly infinite in number and might appear as shadows or misty vapors. They can materialize in forms as tall as a tree, as thin as a blade of grass, or as small as an ant. Spirits might also claim possession of a living person's body, take on human form, or appear as supernatural monsters with razor-sharp teeth.

According to African mythology, there is no place where spirits do not exist; they materialize in every object, creature, and area of earth. Spirits are said to inhabit rock formations, mountains, hills, grasslands, rivers, lakes, clouds, and other natural objects. There are spirits that live throughout the forests and others that live only in certain types of trees. For example, traditional Yoruba believe that a specific group of spirits lives only in the leaves of the sacred Akoko tree. These spirits chatter like birds in the dead of night. Worshippers honor the Akoko spirits by leaving offerings at the foot of the tree and calling out prayers when passing by the tree.

Upstanding Ancestor Spirits

Human-like ancestor spirits, called *egungun* by the Yoruba, differ from the nature spirits referred to as orishas. *Egungun* are concerned with individual morals and the social order. In this role the ancestor spirits act as individual guardians. The *egungun* of deceased parents, grandparents, great-grandparents, and so on, are venerated in many ways. People build shrines in their homes to honor the *egungun*. Villagers form secret organizations, called *egungun* societies, to hold festivals and perform dances wearing masks modeled on respected ancestors.

A Yoruba egungun ritual mask. Egungun are spirits concerned with individual morals and the social order.

Another type of human spirit in African mythology is a spirit twin that acts as a person's double. Among the Isoko and Urhobo of Nigeria, it is said that each newborn is given its own twin guardian spirit that is responsible for its well-being. According to Nigerian religious studies professor E. Bolaji Idowu: "[The spiritual double] is bound up with the issues of a man's destiny on earth; that is, destiny depends on how far this entity is in a good state itself. . . . [It] guards one's steps and brings prosperity, or else it puts obstacles in one's paths. A husband's double may make or mar his wife's fortune; a father's or a mother's [affects] the children."[29]

To ensure good luck, people make sacrifices and offerings to their spirit doubles. If a wife is having a bad time, she might also make an offering to her husband's spirit double.

African mythology also defines spirits of the dead who are not ancestors. Some of these spirits are respected members of a community and venerated by everyone as if they were deceased relatives. Such spirits might include long-dead kings and queens, shamans, and other notable officials. These spirits are often credited with peace, prosperity, and the well-being of the entire community.

Unsettled Spirits

Not all ancestor spirits are seen in a positive light. Some are considered dangerous because they miss their relatives and wish for the living to die and join them in the sky. According to mythological belief, this can sometimes cause newborns to die. It is believed when a grandparent dies around the same time a baby is born, the elder's spirit visits the baby and lures it into the heavenly realm. To prevent this from happening, there are many African rituals meant to protect newborns from recently deceased relatives. Defensive rituals include animal sacrifice, amulets filled with protective herbs, and acts such as swaddling a baby in white cloth, which is symbolic of spiritual purity, sacredness, and joy.

Younger ancestor spirits, which materialize from those who die violently, are also said to cause multiple problems. These spirits are unable to understand that death has occurred. They become frustrated and angry because they

The Diabolical Biloko

African mythology is filled with malicious spirits who appear as hideous monsters. These spirits are said to miss their daily lives and be resentful of the living. Such is the case with the Biloko, diabolical dwarf-like spirits said to inhabit the dense rain forests of the Congo. According to ancient legends, the hairless Biloko dress in leaves and have long claws and pig-like snouts. The fiendish spirits live in hollow trees and cast spells on anyone who dares to enter their jungle domain. The Biloko jealously guard their forest and its precious game and rare fruits. Women are said to faint at the sight of the Biloko, and even the bravest hunters run away in fear. Those who are caught by the spirits might be eaten alive; the Biloko can unhinge their jaws to swallow a human being whole.

are ignored by relatives. In such cases unsettled spirits might try to cling to people and places they knew during life. Such spirits can become mischievous or malevolent and cause all manner of heartbreak, chaos, disease, and disaster.

Traditionally, the belief in unsettled entities is said to be particularly strong among war veterans who trace their haunted dreams to the vengeful spirits they killed in combat. To avoid nightmares, a South African Zulu warrior might disembowel his enemy, allowing the spirit to escape. This act is accompanied by an apology to the spirit.

Ghost Spirits and Witches

Some entities of the dead, called ghost spirits, are considered dangerous to anyone who encounters them. Ghost spirits emerge from people who were not given proper funeral rites upon death. Ghost spirits also materialize if a person dies badly, through hanging, drowning, murder, or other violence.

Those who were wicked when alive might wind up as ghost spirits upon death, forced to wander the world because they are excluded from the heavenly home where good spirits go. Whatever their origins, ghost spirits have long been feared because they are said to haunt gloomy regions of the countryside.

Another type of evil spirit is said to reside within the soul of a witch. During black magic ceremonies, witches materialize these maleficent entities and send them out to perform evil errands. The witch's invisible spirit might cause harm to an enemy's body, mind, relatives, or property.

Witches are also said to use "familiars" to carry out their hexes, or curses. Familiars are supernatural beasts that take the form of animals like spotted hyenas, baboons, polecats, weasels, snakes, owls, or bats. Idowu explains the power of witches: "Persons, animals, or birds are believed to be instruments of possession by [witch] spirits of all descriptions. . . . Spirits may cause insanity or diseases, miscarriages in women, or deformity in human beings."[30] Even in the twenty-first century, witches are widely feared in Africa. As professor of religion Elizabeth McAlister writes, "Many people . . . consider incidents of sickness, layoffs, theft, accidents, and death to be the result of spiritual attack [by witches]."[31]

Spiritual Healing

People who believe a witch is causing them harm may consult a spiritual healer. If they are Zulus living in South Africa, they will seek out a male or female shaman called a *sangoma*. Still active today, *sangomas* use divination and magical rituals to heal those suffering from physical, emotional, or spiritual illnesses.

Sangomas practice *ngoma*, a healing method that uses the power of ancestor spirits. The most powerful *sangomas* do not simply take up the trade; they must be chosen by ancestors in dreams or visions. A spirit takes possession of a *sangoma*'s body and uses it as a channel of communication between the physical and spirit realms.

To be chosen by the spirits is considered a gift and a blessing but requires a *sangoma* to undergo arduous training. The *sangoma* must learn to enter a

Spirits and Strikers

In June 2014 striking miners in South Africa enlisted the help of *sangoma* to prevent violence during bloody protests. The *sangoma* called on the spirits to make police guns jam if fired at protesters.

trance state, which often requires the healer to fast and perform extended rituals that involve drumming, chanting, and dancing. Such rituals are performed from dusk until dawn to generate supernatural healing energies within the *sangoma*.

Spirit possession can be painful and dangerous for the *sangoma*. During some intense trance states, healers might attempt to walk through burning coals or slash themselves with sharp objects. Healers can also get lost in the supernatural realm and not be able to find their way back. Anthropologist Pierre Verger explains: "[The *sangoma*] seems to lose all reason, he is plunged into a dazed state of mental paralysis; he has forgotten everything, no longer knows how to speak and talks only in unintelligible sounds."[32] To prevent such problems, *sangomas* are carefully observed by ceremonial singers and drummers, who will calm the music or even stop the ritual if necessary.

Throwing Divination Bones

Because of the dangers associated with trance possession, *sangomas* developed an easier method of healing. They engage in a practice called throwing divination bones. South African medical doctor and *sangoma* researcher David Cumes describes the process:

> The divination bones are an alternative way of allowing the ancestral spirits to have a conversation with the patient through the healer. . . . The healer becomes an interpreter and messenger for the ancestral spirit, who sets up an information "field" accessible to the *sangoma* through the bones. When the bones are thrown by the *sangoma*, they do not fall in a random fashion but in a way that the ancestral spirit controls. A meaningful and usually highly accurate interpretation can be made.[33]

Divination bones are the rounded, rock-like neck and spine bones of various animals. The bones come from lions, hyenas, anteaters, crocodiles, baboons, and livestock such as goats and pigs. The powers of the bones are related to the animals from which they are taken. For example, in African mythology the hyena is often represented as a thief who comes in the night. As such, using a hyena's bones gives the *sangoma*

Spirit Dream Messages

South African healers called sangomas *rely on channeling, possession, and divination to heal clients harmed by evil spirits. Dream interpretation is also used to break hexes and heal the spiritually wounded. South African medical doctor and* sangoma *researcher David Cumes explains:*

According to the *sangomas* and other ancient wisdom, our dream state is every bit as real as the waking state and all we have to do is decipher the cosmic conversation. . . . *Sangomas* dream about patients coming to them and about specific plant remedies for those patients. Even though they may never have seen that plant before, they will go into the bush, find it, and then dispense it. *Sangomas* appreciate that these spirit dream messages usually occur in the early hours of the morning. They say this is when the ancestors are active. . . .

The *sangoma* is always confronting opposition from witches, sorcerers and intrusive spirits from the other side. They can access the *sangoma's* dreamtime and all dreams are liable to pollution from trickster spirits. The [dream] field, like the Internet, is impartial to messages, light or dark, both have free access. Just as there are viruses, Trojan horses, pornographic pop ups etc. on the web so there are dark energies in the spirit world that want to corrupt the *sangoma's* dream files.

David Cumes. "South African Indigenous Healing: How It Works." *Explore*, January 2013. www.explorejournal.com/article/S1550-8307(12)00225-X/fulltext#sec1.

South African healers called sangomas *rely on channeling, possession, and divination to heal people harmed by evil spirits.*

the power to locate stolen objects. The anteater is said to dig a grave with its long tongue, and its bones are used for divination when a deceased spirit is involved. Divination bones might also include shells, seeds, money, dice, or dominoes, each with its own meaning.

When throwing divination bones, the *sangoma* first calls up an ancestor, claps the hands, shakes a rattle, and sings a song. The healer poses questions for the spirit to answer and throws the bones after each query. The distinct arrangement of the bones when they fall is interpreted by the *sangoma*. According to Cumes, the *sangoma* does not attempt to push a specific answer upon the client:

A South African sangoma uses bones, shells, and pebbles to communicate with spirits of the ancestors.

> The information is given humbly and democratically. The healer will ask the patient if she agrees and, if so, will continue along the same line of exploration. If the patient disagrees, the healer will read another polarity [alignment of the bones] or look at the same polarity in a different way. . . . The bones will often highlight or focus on a problem that requires attention and that may have been ignored or denied.[34]

When establishing contact with ancestor spirits and channeling their knowledge, *sangomas* are communicating with the dead. The healers voluntarily offer their bodies and minds as vessels for spirit possession. To be chosen for such a role is seen as a high honor and blessing, as Cumes explains: "Every one of us would welcome having a loving mentor who bestows gifts and can see and understand things that normally elude us."[35]

Among the Kongo people of central Africa only women are allowed to enter into trance states for purposes of divination.

Possessed Women

Sangomas are both male and female. But among the Kongo people of central Africa, only women are allowed to enter into trance states for divination. This follows the Kongo belief that females are most strongly associated with spirit communications, especially twins; the most revered women shamans are twins, mothers of twins, or females born to twins. This can be traced to the powers associated with twins found throughout African mythology. Twins are central to many creation stories and often symbolize both perfection and disaster. It is said twins bring double of everything, both good and bad. Twins are twice as painful to birth but generate twice as much good luck for their parents.

Whatever the sibling status of the shaman, Kongo women engage in ecstatic communications with the spirits in order

Water Spirits

The *jengu* are beautiful mermaid-like water spirits said to live in the rivers of Cameroon. The *jengu* bring good luck to those who worship them and cure diseases by enlisting the help of other cosmic spirits.

to explore cosmic truths about the past, present, and future. Their work features strong elements of public performance.

Kongo shamans only perform divination rites at night, when the dead are said to be awake and closer to the physical world. Unlike *sangomas* and others who perform extended rituals, Kongo mystics enter trance states suddenly, sometimes within minutes. The process is marked by shouts, shrieks, and outbursts of song by the shaman. She can also make cacophonous, or harsh-sounding, music with whistles, gongs, and bells. In addition, the shaman will spit on observers, since the Kongo believe her saliva is a blessing and a show of divine power.

Revealing Information

After a spirit makes itself known, friends and relatives in attendance ask it to identify itself. An ancestor who refuses to do so is considered unreliable and unwelcome. Once identified, the spirit is asked the purpose of its visit. There are three possible answers: The spirit appears as a courtesy to the shaman, it is there to report on the family's welfare, or it has important information to reveal. The welfare of the family is perhaps the most important aspect because it is believed that the ancestor can protect the health and well-being of the living relatives. Ancestors might warn of an impending illness or diagnose a sick person, providing instructions for an herbal remedy.

During Kongo rituals, an ancestor sometimes discloses that evil spirits are approaching. When receiving this news, the shaman will walk toward the harmful entity or point in its direction. In some cases the shaman will try to fight off the wicked spirit by arguing with it or even engaging in physical battle. During such episodes the woman may enter a crazed state, shouting, flailing her limbs about, and throwing objects at the invisible enemy. The shaman might speak in tongues; that is, utter unintelligible phrases said to be spirit communications. The Kongo believe these words are heavenly languages with the power to ward off wickedness.

The Kongo divination ceremony ends when the shaman repeats the warnings and recommendations of the spirit. At this time, gathered family members promise that they will never forget the visitation and ask the spirit to send love to other ancestors living in the cosmos. Finally, the shaman waves good-bye to the spirit with both hands, indicating the session is over. After the ceremony shamans often fall into a deep sleep and cannot remember what happened when they awake.

Although Kongo trance ceremonies require little preparation, some foods are associated with the divination rituals. Palm wine is poured on the shaman when she enters a state of ecstasy. This symbolizes richness, fertility, and honor. Ground

Witches Work Havoc

Evil spirits have long been associated with witchcraft in African mythology. The Yoruba associate witches and sorcerers with the term aiyé, *which means "the world." In this usage, the term defines the concentrated essence of all the diabolical, malignant, and spoiled aspects of the world. Nigerian religious studies professor E. Bolaji Idowu examines the role of spirits in witchcraft:*

It is generally believed that the guild of witches have their regular meetings and ceremonies in forests or in open places in the middle of the night. The meeting is the meeting of the "souls," "spirits," of the witches. In several places in Africa, it is believed that the spirits leave the bodies of witches in [the] form of a particular kind of bird. Their main purpose is to work havoc on other human beings; and the operation is the operation of spirits upon spirits, that is, it is the ethereal bodies of the victims that are attacked, extracted, and devoured; and this is what is meant when it is said that witches have sucked the entire blood of the victim. Thus, in the case of witches or their victims, spirits meet spirits, spirits operate upon spirits, while the actual human bodies lie "asleep" in their homes.

E. Bolaji Idowu. *African Traditional Religion*. Maryknoll, NY: Orbis, 1973, p. 176.

kola nuts are sprinkled on the shaman to enhance her mystical connection. During a visitation, observers sprinkle salt around the house to ward off evil spirits.

Drumming Up Spirits

In African mythology all drums are considered to contain their own spirits and the spirits of those who made them.

Although the Kongo use bells, gongs, and whistles during rituals, drums have long been at the center of African spirit communication. Archaeologists have discovered African drums more than twenty thousand years old in ancient settlements. These instruments made from animal skulls, skins, antlers, bones, seashells, and wood were considered sacred and used by shamans during rituals and ceremonies.

In African mythology the drum of the Venda of South Africa is known as the Drum of the Dead. It is regarded as the voice of Mwali, the ancestor god, and its sound is said to strike fear in the hearts of enemies. Traditionally, only the highest shaman or king was allowed to see or play the drum. The large drum was kept in a box that required six couriers to move it. In one legend the Drum of the Dead was being transported but was dropped. It fell out of the box and onto the ground. As punishment, Mwali unleashed a horrific storm while releasing hundreds of vicious lions to kill people.

Not all drums are as significant as the Drum of the Dead, but all are considered to contain their own spirits and the spirits of those who made them. Traditionally, when African artisans made drums, they first made an offering to the spirit of the tree they cut down for the wood. The tree spirits lived on, inhabiting the drum. A second drum spirit was related to the female goat, deer, camel, or zebra whose skin was used to make the drumhead.

Drum-making traditions remain alive in Africa today, and many drums are made with ropes attached to the drumhead. When these ropes are squeezed under the arm, the drum changes tone. This manipulation allows drummers to make drums "talk." Specific drumbeats are like phrases that are understood by listeners who know the same language. In addition to sending spirit messages, drum spirits are credited with making people get up and dance and for facilitating trances.

Masked Dancers

Led by the drum, spirit dances often involve entire communities. These events, accompanied by chanting, storytelling, and singing, are held to honor seasonal spirits or celebrate spirits involved with rites of passage such as marriages, births, or funerals.

Dances might be led by a shaman or members of an elite group such as the Egungun Society. In some cases dancers don spectacular masks designed to appeal to forces beyond the physical world. During extended rituals, mask

A Punu dance mask is worn by stilt dancers in some African funeral ceremonies.

wearers enter into trances or dreamlike states. This allows them to act as conduits between the physical and spiritual worlds and relay messages from the spirits. Traditionally, the masks used in such rituals are viewed as sacred and powerful. Apart from community dances, the masks are kept hidden from view. Oftentimes even their meaning and powers remain unknown to the general public.

Among the Punu people of Gabon, mask rituals were developed as a vital way to neutralize evil forces. Punu rituals are led by men belonging to a society called *mukudj.*

They perform rites wearing masks of beautiful women that represent nature spirits. The masks are painted white, a color representing peace, lightness, and beauty. Because they represent idealized Punu femininity, the masks have pursed lips, protruding eyes, high foreheads, and elaborate traditional hairstyles. The masks also show diamond-shaped facial scars, which Punu women view as signs of beauty.

In rituals, *mukudj* representing the female spirits dance on long stilts nearly 9 feet (2.7m) high. Dancers train from childhood so they can master the complex choreography while perched on the stilts. It is believed that those who exhibit the strength, agility, and balance necessary for stilt dancing are drawing on mystical powers. This places mask dancers in an unusual light. Although they are admired by the community, they might also be regarded warily as shamans who make secret alliances with dark spirits.

In the twenty-first century, the mask dance of the Punu is still performed, as both a religious celebration and a tourist attraction, which is a point of national pride in Gabon. And although the masks were once kept hidden, many are now displayed in museums such as the National Museum of African Art in Washington, D.C. Masks dating from the the nineteenth century are extremely valuable to art collectors, and in 2012, a mask made in the late 1800s sold at auction for more than four hundred thousand dollars.

Masks, drums, dances, and trances have been intertwined with spirit possession for millennia. For those who engage in traditional African religious practices, such as the dancers, diviners, *sangomas*, and Kongo, the spirits remain alive in modern times. And even in the twenty-first century, traditional practices continue to influence African belief.

According to an extensive 2010 poll by the Pew Research Center, one-third of all Africans believe that sacrifices to ancestors or spirits can protect them from harm. About one-quarter of Africans say they believe in the protective powers of amulets, shrines, and other sacred objects. One-third of those polled had contacted a traditional healer when a family member was sick. In some countries the numbers were higher; in Senegal traditional beliefs were held by three out of four citizens.

Acceptance of African mythology exists alongside strong belief in Christianity and Islam, two religions practiced by more than 90 percent of Africans. But the ancient beliefs remain strong and endure because of the power behind the traditions, rituals, dances, and artwork of African mythology that have been handed down for generations.

CHAPTER 5

Ancient Beliefs in the New World

African mythology is filled with stories about nightmarish journeys across churning seas and evil entities committing unspeakable acts. For example, an ancient Kongo legend describes a hero who is unwittingly transported to the realm of Mputu, a place of agitated waters and shadowy forces of evil.

Although the origins of the Mputu story are unclear, the plot may be a reference to the European slave trade. As Clyde W. Ford explains, the agitated waters are "an allusion both to the Atlantic surf out of which Europeans appeared and into which Africans disappeared. . . . Slaves were heroes, thrust into the bleak landscape of Mputu to confront the dark powers there."[36]

The hero of the Kongo legend eventually finds civilization, food, and other necessities. But this was not the case for West African men, women, and children brought to the New World as slaves. People from all classes of society were violently separated from their friends, family, villages, and culture. Thus stripped of their identity, Africans were auctioned as chattel in slave markets. There was little chance of conquest over the slavers and no escaping the sugar, cotton, and coffee plantations where Africans toiled under unimaginably brutal conditions.

West African men, women, and children were kidnapped and brought to Haiti, where they were sold in slave markets.

Vodun to Voodoo

During the eighteenth century, around half a million West African slaves were brought to the French-ruled island of Haiti, then known as Saint-Domingue. The Africans belonged to various ethnic groups, but most were people of Fon, Ewe, Kongo, and Yoruba descent. They came from the coastal regions of West Africa called the Kingdom of Dahomey, an area that included parts of present-day Benin and Togo.

Some of the slaves were priestesses, sorcerers, herbalists, and tribal chiefs schooled in the ways of spirit magic and ancient tribal mythology. Although they were forced to leave their homeland behind, the shamans brought their oral traditions with them. In the new land they resurrected their religious beliefs in secret and kept alive the deities and spirits they had known at home. Since most slaves were Dahomean, the African mythology took on the name *vodun*, which means "spirit" in Fon. Eventually the word *vodou* (or *voodoo*) came to define the ancient African religion practiced in New World.

French slavers strictly forbade slaves from practicing voodoo, under penalty of whipping, beating, or death. In addition, the slave owners imposed Christianity on the Africans. According to a 1665 decree, slaves on Saint-Domingue were required to be "baptized and instructed in the Catholic . . . religion. Residents who buy newly-arrived slaves . . . will give the necessary orders for the baptism and instruction of the slaves."[37] As a result of this decree, thousands of Haitian slaves were baptized, attended mass, and learned about Catholic saints.

The Master, the Gatekeeper, and the Goddess

Throughout the eighteenth century black Haitians merged numerous ancient African deities and spirits with Catholic saints. This created what anthropologists call Afro-Haitian saints. The chief voodoo god was viewed much the same way Christians behold the God of the Bible. Voodooists believe the deity, Grande Maître or Gran Mèt (Grand Master), created the world and everything in it. Gran Mèt also shares characteristics with Yoruba creator deity Olorun. Like Olorun, Gran Mèt is too glorious to bother with the mundane daily desires of human beings. This led him to create hundreds of spirits called *loa* (or *lwa*) to deal with people on an individual basis.

Legba, or Papa Legba, was the first and most important *loa* created by Gran Mèt. Papa Legba acts as an intermediary, or gatekeeper, between humanity and all other *loas*. Legba is called the master of the crossroads and is identified with Saint Peter, who is said to stand at the gates of heaven. Before voodooists can address any *loa*, they must

Voodoo in the USA

During the 1960s and 1970s, Haitians fleeing repression in their homeland migrated to Miami, New York City, and Chicago and brought their voodoo beliefs with them.

petition Legba to open the gate between the physical and cosmic worlds. At the start of any voodoo ritual, these words are spoken: "Papa Legba, open the gate for me. Legba, open the gates so we may pass through. Papa; When I will have passed, I thank the loa. . . . Legba who sits on the gate, Give us the right to pass."[38] Legba not only opens the cosmic gate, he is also the guardian of the gates and fences that safeguard homes. As a protector of roads, he safeguards travelers and wards off evil spirits that haunt the highways.

Like many male *loa*, Legba has a female counterpart. Erzulie, also known as Ezili-Freda-Dahomeym, is the goddess of love. Erzulie shares traits with the Christian Virgin Mary; she is idealized as a symbol of feminine perfection. Erzulie embodies beauty, tenderness, and passion. However, unlike the Virgin Mary, Erzulie is not celebrated for her abstinence but for her skills in love.

Erzulie is said to have unlimited riches and access to grand luxuries. She wears gold jewelry, expensive clothes, and fine perfume. Supplicants hoping to win Erzulie's favor hold ceremonies with displays of fine foods, expen-

A Papa Legba shrine in New Orleans, Louisiana. Papa Legba acts as an intermediary, or gatekeeper, between humanity and all other loas, *or spirits.*

sive soaps and perfumes, embroidered towels, and jewels. When female or male voodooists are possessed by Erzulie, they dress in her clothes and take on the role of a seductive love goddess.

The Snake and the Corpse

The serpent god Damballah is another important *loa*. Damballah is associated with Saint Patrick, who drove the snakes out of Ireland and is often pictured with serpents. Known as the Good Serpent of the Sky, Damballah is represented as a snake traveling the arc that the sun makes across the sky during the day. The stars in the sky are Damballah's coils. He is said to live in the heavenly tree of wisdom, but in his grandeur he does not impart his knowledge to humanity.

Damballah is responsible for the life-giving rains that sustain humankind; he created water when he shed his skin. The voodoo serpent is also symbolized by things that represent the beauty of nature, including melons, pineapples, bananas, oranges, desserts, sweet liqueurs, and flowers. Damballah is associated with eggs, bones, ivory, and the color white. He is the protector of the young, the helpless, and the disabled. Those who make regular offerings to Damballah hope for good luck on a grand scale, expecting to become wealthy, powerful, and strong. The serpent's female counterpart, Ayida, is the rainbow. Together the two *loas* symbolize the union of man and woman.

As the life giver, Damballah stands in opposition to the *loa* Ghede, whose domain includes death, cemeteries, and the end of time. Ghede is represented by darkness and the abyss. He dresses completely in black like an undertaker, with a long coat, a top hat, and dark glasses. Ghede lingers at the crossroads of death, where all people must cross one day. In this role Ghede represents the inevitable end of life.

Ghede's symbols include skulls, bones, the black wooden cross, the pickax and shovel of the grave digger, and piles of stones representing gravestones. Rooms set aside for him at ceremonies are ghoulish in appearance. They contain sacrificial offerings, including a strong rum spiked with twenty-one habañero peppers, one of the hottest spices in the world. The drink is so peppery only Ghede himself can swallow it.

Practitioners who take on the spirit of the cigar-chomping Ghede tell shocking but false sexual stories about community members. They taunt listeners and embarrass them with the foulest language while gesturing obscenely. This breaking of taboos—common in death mythology of African cultures—is said to represent the sinner in all people.

Spirits and Ceremonies

Practitioners of voodoo consult with Ghede, Damballah, Erzulie, Legba, and countless other *loas* before engaging in important matters concerning love, marriage, money, luck, and controlling enemies. To do so, voodooists engage in practices that would be familiar to ancient Africans. They pray, sing, play drums, and dance until they enter the hypnotic state of the possession trance. During this activity, the *loa* are said to enter the bodies of the voodooists and ride them like horses. When the spirits take hold, people implore the gods for various favors. In 1797 French writer M.L.E. Moreau de Saint-Méry wrote the first account of a voodoo ceremony and described the desires of the petitioners:

> Most slaves ask for the ability to direct the thoughts of their masters. But this is not enough. One begs for money. Another seeks the gift of pleasing a girl who will pay no attention to him. This one wishes to call back an unfaithful mistress, that one asks to be made well or to have a longer life. After them, an old woman wants to implore God to stop the scorn of someone whose happy youth she would capture. A young girl asks for everlasting love—or repeats the wishes that hatred dictates to her as to a preferred rival.[39]

The eighteenth-century desires expressed for money, love, and health differ little from what is heard at voodoo ceremonies today. At least 60 million people practice the syncretic religion in Haiti, the United States, and elsewhere.

Voodoo in 1797

In 1797 Haitian voodooists allowed sympathetic French writer M.L.E. Moreau de Saint-Méry to attend one of their ceremonies. He wrote the first detailed description of voodoo and its rituals:

[Voodooists believe in Damballah,] an all-powerful, supernatural being. Upon this being hang all the events which occur on this globe. Now this being is a snake, not of a poisonous kind, often an adder. It is under the adder's auspices that the believers assemble. Knowledge of the past, learning of the present, and foreknowledge of the future are all attributed to this snake. The adder is never willing to share its power, or to tell its wishes except through the medium of a high priest [or King] chosen by the cult members. Later, a woman participates; a negress whom the love of this latter person has raised to the rank of high priestess [or Queen].

The King puts his hand or his foot on the adder's cage and soon is possessed. He then transmits this mood to the Queen, who in turn passes it on to those in the circle. Each makes movements, in which the upper part of the body, the head and shoulders, seem to be dislocated. The Queen above all is the prey to the most violent agitations. From time to time she goes up to the Voodoo snake to seek some new magic and shakes the chest and the little bells with which it is adorned, making them ring out in a very climax or folly. But the delirium keeps rising. . . . Faintings and raptures take over some of them and a sort of fury some of the others, but for all there is a nervous trembling which they cannot master. They spin around ceaselessly.

Quoted in Roy Rosenzweig Center for History and New Media. "Voodoo." https://chnm.gmu.edu/revolution/d/336/.

A bas-relief of the Good Serpent of the Sky, Damballah, the all-powerful voodoo god..

Rada and Petro

The *loas* of voodoo are divided into two main spirit families, Rada and Petro, derived from Yoruba mythology. The two groups contrast with one another. Rada spirits are cool, sweet, calm, and peaceful. Petro spirits are hot, bitter, aggressive, and restless. Rada *loas* are seen as family members whose characteristics are familiar and comforting. They surround believers with personal protection on a daily basis. Petro *loas* are viewed as outsiders and foreigners, fierce and stubborn, who must be treated with great caution. Voodooists do not break promises or bend the rules when dealing with Petro *loas*.

The term *Rada* connects Haitians to their African homeland. The word is derived from the town Arada in Dahomey.

The elaborate rites associated with these spirits most closely resemble those of West African mythology. Among the gods in the Rada pantheon are Legba, Erzulie, Damballah, and Ghede.

The term *Petro* is obscure, but some believe it is derived from the dance of Don Pedro. The frantic voodoo dance, which originated in the Congo, was named after an eighteenth-century Spanish voodoo priest named Jean-Philippe Pedro. Traditionally, those performing the Dance of Don Pedro drink rum mixed with gunpowder. This propels their convulsive movements into a state of madness that sometimes results in heart failure. Like the bizarre Don Pedro dance, Petro *loas* are honored with rowdy behavior that includes fire, gunpowder explosions, cracking whips, and shrieking whistles.

Unlike the individualistic Rada *loa*, Petro spirits tend to look and act alike and represent only about 5 percent of voodoo deities. In their anonymity the spirits signify hot tempers, violent behavior, war, bad deeds, and black magic. Some believe the Petro spirits are an expression of rage against slavery, a way for captive Haitians to seize the power held by their oppressors and use it against them.

With two contrasting pantheons, people need a divine intermediary when dealing with the Rada and Petro *loas*. Consequently, voodooists who need to make wrenching life decisions consult with the deity Ogou, the Haitian version of Ogun, the Yoruba god of iron. Ogou is very virile, a perfect example of manhood. He is the *loa* of iron, lightning, and war. In this role Ogou has the strength, wisdom, and power to guide a devotee toward a cool Rada *loa* or a hot Petro *loa* to solve any vexing problem.

Santeria: The Way of the Saints

Ogou plays a similar role in Santeria, another syncretic religion that blends African beliefs with those forged in the New World. With his roots in Ogun, the Santeria Ogou is a mighty warrior and cosmic blacksmith who crafts tools, weapons, and the sharpest knives.

Ogou is a *loa* in Haiti but is called an *oricha* in Cuba, where Santeria developed. *Oricha* is the Spanish term for

Devotees of Spiritism

A religious belief called *Espiritismo*, or Spiritism in English, developed in Cuba in the nineteenth century. Devotees of *Espiritismo* blend elements of Santeria, voodoo, and Catholicism and believe good and evil spirits can affect luck, love, health, and other aspects of life.

semidivine Santeria beings, usually spelled *orisha*. The word is derived from *orisa*, the term for Yoruba spirits. In Spanish, *Santeria* means "honor of the saints" or "way of the saints." Male devotees are called santeros, and females are called santeras. The liturgical language used by Santeria priests and priestesses is Lucumi, a dialect of the south Nigerian Yoruba people.

As with voodoo, Santeria developed among African slaves in the New World and is syncretized with Catholic saints. Devotees of both faiths practice animal sacrifice in the belief it will give life to the dead and provide food for the spirits. However, voodooists do not practice sacrifice on as large a scale as Santeria worshippers.

There are differences between the two belief systems: Santeria is mainly influenced by Yoruba belief, whereas voodoo draws not only from the Yoruba but from the Fon, Ewe, and Kongo practices as well. Both share an organized hierarchy of spirits, but there are seven main Santeria orishas, compared to twelve principal voodoo *loas*. And voodoo is considered an official religion in Haiti, whereas Santeria is not recognized by the government of Cuba. However, Santeria has gained visibility in the United States, especially in Florida and New York, where many Cuban refugees live.

The supreme creator god in Santeria is referred to by three Yoruba-based names: Olorun, Olodumare, and Olofi. Mirroring the Christian Holy Trinity of the Father, Son, and Holy Ghost, the Santeria creator is seen as three aspects of the same thing. Olorun is the originator and creator of being, Olodumare is the divine essence of all there is, and Olofi is the creation itself, he who dwells in all creation.

Drumming Up the Orishas

Santeria rituals allow followers to engage in communication with the orishas, who are the messengers of the gods on earth. As with other African-based belief systems, Santeria ceremonies include long periods of drumming, dancing, chanting, singing, and trance possession.

At drum ceremonies, called *tambor*, three sacred drums are played. The two-headed drums, which are large, medium, and small, produce a variety of tones central to Santeria worship. Devotees believe that each orisha has a unique musical rhythm and tone, called a *toque*, or beat. When properly played by highly trained Santeria drummers, a *toque* calls a specific orisha down to earth.

A Santeria shrine in Cuba. Santeria developed among African slaves in the New World and is syncretized with Catholic devotion to saints.

When Santeria ceremonies begin, devotees address Eleguá, the Santeria version of Papa Legba. Eleguá is a trickster who opens the doors of communication between the orishas and the worshippers. Santeria priestess Cynthia Duncan describes what happens next:

> The Santeros, in order of seniority, salute the drums by doing the *foribale*, a formal gesture that requires them to prostrate themselves by lying on the floor in front of the drums for a few seconds. Then, they must salute each drum individually by touching their forehead to it while the drum is playing. . . . Seniority is important during the dancing segments of the ritual. Elders must always be closest to the drums.[40]

As the drumming ritual continues, Santeria devotees fall into trances. Like voodooists, they believe the spirits are riding them like horses and speaking through them. The orishas usually mount the worshippers one by one. When the crowd sees a devotee overtaken—turning into a *caballo* (horse)—they gather around, praise the orisha, and offer encouragement to come down. According to Duncan, "Sometimes the possession can appear traumatic, even violent. The one possessed may fall to the floor and begin to shake, or run around the room in a disoriented state."[41]

Some *caballos* identify with the orisha Shangó (or Changó), the spirit of thunder, lightning, and drumming. When drummers play a *toque* for Shangó, the devotee will become possessed. In such a case the *caballo* is taken out of the room and dressed in ceremonial attire symbolic of Shangó. The garb includes red satin pants, a red blouse with white trim, a sword, and a crown. The possessed person, whether male or female, may imitate Shangó's characteristics. These are described by Duncan: "He knows how to be a good friend, he's a master at divination, and he's a great healer. But . . . he's a great womanizer, and a bit of a [freethinker]. He seduces with his charm and his lies. He's a fast

Santeria Dance Rhythms

In Cuba Santeria rhythms have long been played in a secularized form called rumba, a passionate and rhythmic dance music that includes improvised lyrics about street life, politics, and humorous events.

A tambor
drum used to
communicate with
the orishas during a
Santeria ceremony.

talker, and can be manipulative. He can also be a compulsive
gambler and wasteful with money. When his ego gets out of
control, he's arrogant and domineering."[42]

Shangó is one of several spirits that can take possession
of Santeria followers. Other major orishas include Yemayá,
the ruler of the seas; Obatala, the creator of earth and the
sculptor of humankind; and Oshún, the ruler of the rivers
and the essence of love.

Spirit possession usually ends when dawn breaks and the drums fall silent. At this time *caballos* are escorted by the nonpossessed from the ceremonial site and urged to lie down and rest. Freed from the orishas, the possessed return to normal consciousness.

Spirits in Stones

It is said that all Santeria orishas possess a spiritual and magical energy called *aché*, which is found throughout the universe. Devotees believe no life would exist without *aché*. The energy encompasses all knowledge, divine grace, authority, strength, and the human life force. According to Duncan, "It's impossible to define aché in more concrete terms because it's a metaphysical concept that by its very nature escapes definition. It's too complex for the human mind to fully grasp. No matter how we try to describe it or imagine it, it will exceed the limits of our minds."[43]

Aché was created by Olorun and spread throughout the earth by the orishas when they descended from heaven at the beginning of creation. The indefinable energy was left behind in certain stones, which vibrate with the *aché* of the orishas. The stones are central to Santeria worship, as Brooklyn-based santero Joseph M. Murphy explains: "Devotees can find these *orisha* stones among ordinary ones if they can learn to listen carefully enough. For the *orisha* stones are alive with the *orisha*'s *aché*. They are most likely to be found in the element most expressive of their force—ocean stones for Yemayá, river pebbles for Oshún, meteorites for the thunder king Shangó."[44]

The stones are the seen as vibrant symbols of the orishas on earth. They are venerated and treated with great respect as if they were living beings. The stones are bathed in pure waters containing herbs associated with specific orishas. These holy infusions not only clean the stones but are said to channel healing powers to devotees by focusing the *aché*. When stones are removed from the baths, they are dried, rubbed with fragrant oils, and sometimes sprayed with expensive perfumes. Most important, the stones are fed with the blood of sacrificed animals.

Voodoo in New Orleans

In the early 1800s thousands of Haitians immigrated to New Orleans, Louisiana, and brought their voodoo practices with them. In later years, voodoo became an important element of the city.

Part religious belief and part tourist attraction, slaves and free blacks gathered in the New Orleans Congo Square every Sunday to play drums and perform traditional voodoo dances. The scene attracted many wealthy whites, especially women,

Visitors to New Orleans can stop and see Marie Leveau's House of Voodoo on Bourbon Street.

who were drawn to voodoo practices. The high-society women often hired voodoo priests and priestesses to predict the future, read minds, cast spells, remove curses, and make magical potions.

A few voodooists grew rich and famous due to their work with their white patrons. The most renowned was a free black woman named Marie Laveau, who began her career in the 1830s as a hairdresser for wealthy society ladies. As she worked, Laveau listened to her customers gossiping and made note of their many "secrets." When she was consulted as a voodoo priestess, she was able to use the notes to describe clients' problems with startling accuracy. After she became famous, Laveau hired spies—black servants in white households—to gather dirt about love affairs, business dealings, illnesses, and other useful information.

With her wealth, beauty, and theatrical flair, Laveau was called the "Queen of the Saints." Her most famous attraction was her Sunday snake dance at Congo Square. An ex-slave, Tom Bragg, described the scene: "When she got through dancin'. . . . She could make anybody do anything and sometimes she made 'em do terrible things. She made people disappear. She made wives turn on their husbands and run off wit' other men. She made fine white ladies lie on the ground and roll on their bellies."

Quoted in Robert Tallant. *Voodoo in New Orleans.* Gretna, LA: Pelican, 1994, p. 57.

Blood Sacrifice

During sacrifice ceremonies, holy stones are placed in sacred pots called *soperas* that resemble soup tureens. Each orisha has its own kind of *sopera*. For example, Shangó's is always wooden and elevated on a small wooden stool. This is due to Shangó's legend, which states that he had a violent dispute with the iron god Ogou. As a result, all Shangó shrines and symbols are of wood, the opposite of iron. Conversely, Ogou's *sopera* is an iron cauldron with three little legs.

During some Santeria rituals, the throats of animals such as chickens, roosters, goats, and sheep are slit with a sharp knife. (This method is considered humane and is identical to the way animals are handled during Jewish kosher and Islamic halal religious slaughter.) The blood is drained from the animal and used to feed the stones in the *sopera*. Murphy explains the use of blood sacrifice: "The *orishas*, like all living things, must eat. . . . [The blood of the animals] is offered to *orishas* to show human beings their dependence on the world outside them and to give back to the invisible world something of what it gives to the visible."[45]

The animals do not go to waste; they are cooked and eaten by the community after the ceremony concludes. The orishas eat the blood, the humans eat the meat, and there is a communion with the spirits.

Living Mythology

The influence of African mythology in the New World is powerful and profound. In Brazil practitioners of Candomblé mix Yoruba, Fon, Ewe, and Bantu beliefs with Catholicism and use chanting, drumming, and dance to enable worshippers to be possessed by the orishas. The rhythms of Candomblé have influenced popular Brazilian music genres since the late nineteenth century. The sounds can be heard in Brazil's famed samba and bossa nova music, and these beats strongly influenced rock, hip-hop, funk, and other modern musical styles.

West African voodoo mythology has also had a profound impact on modern culture, particularly when the subject is zombies. The idea of an undead spirit walking the earth

while terrorizing the living originated among the Kongo. In Haiti zombies have long been feared as corpses that have been animated through black magic.

Although they are a minor aspect of voodoo belief, zombies have gripped the public imagination since author William B. Seabrook described them in his book *The Magic Island* in 1929. Since that time zombies have starred in countless books, films, and television shows.

The best-selling 2006 zombie novel *World War Z* by Max Brooks was turned into a blockbuster film of the same name starring Brad Pitt in 2013. The zombie series *The Walking Dead* was a top-selling graphic novel and a hit TV show that premiered in 2010. Zombie-themed video games such as *Resident Evil*, *Doom*, and *House of the Dead* are a

Voodoo zombies have always intrigued people but are particularly trendy in the pop culture of the second decade of the twenty-first century.

billion-dollar industry, and stores sell around $500 million worth of zombie costumes every Halloween.

While the zombie fad might seem trivial, there is little doubt that ancient African concepts such as ritual drumming and dancing, black magic, divination, and spirit possession have long influenced other cultures. With roots stretching back to the early evolution of humanity, traditional African mythology remains alive and continues to grip humanity with ancient beliefs that still hold power.

NOTES

Introduction: The Way of the Ancestors

1. Elizabeth Isichei. *The Religious Traditions of Africa: A History*. Westport, CT: Praeger, 2004, p. 4.
2. Isichei. *The Religious Traditions of Africa*, p. 4.
3. Ngwabi Bhebe. *Christianity and Traditional Religion in Western Zimbabwe, 1859–1923*. London: Longman, 1979, p. 53.
4. Carol Beckwith and Angela Fischer. *African Ceremonies*. Vol. 2. New York: Abrams, 1999, p. 237.
5. Harold Scheub. *African Mythology: The Mythmaker as Storyteller*. Oxford: Oxford University Press, 2000, p. xi.

Chapter 1: Myths, Cultures, and Kingdoms

6. Quoted in E.A. Wallis Budge. *An Introduction to Ancient Egyptian Literature*. Mineola, NY: Dover, 1997, p. 214.
7. Sandra T. Barnes and Paula Girshick Ben-Amos. *Africa's Ogun, Old World and New*. Bloomington: Indiana University Press, 1997, p. 2.

8. Stephen Adebanji Akintoye. *A History of the Yoruba People*. Dakar, Senegal: Amalion, 2010, p. 19.
9. Akintoye. *A History of the Yoruba People*, p. 35.
10. William Bascom. *Ifa Divination*. Bloomington: Indiana University Press, 1969, p. 61.

Chapter 2: Creation Myths

11. J.B. Danquah. *The Akan Doctrine of God: A Fragment of Gold Coast Ethics and Religion*. London: Routledge, 1968, p. 21.
12. Harry Sawyer. *God: Ancestor or Creator?* London: Longmans, 1970, p. 40.
13. Clyde W. Ford. *The Hero with an African Face*. New York: Bantam, 2000, p. 188.
14. Ford. *The Hero with an African Face*, p. 188.
15. Quoted in Asar Imhotep. "The Esoteric Science of Spittin." Mujilu, November 23, 2010. https://asarimhotep.com/documentdownloads/theesotericscienceofspittin.pdf.
16. Quoted in Ford. *The Hero with an African Face*, p. 182.
17. Quoted in Ford. *The Hero with an African Face*, p. 178.

18. Quoted in Ford. *The Hero with an African Face*, p. 172.
19. Quoted in Benjamin C. Ray. *African Religions*. Upper Saddle River, NJ: Prentice Hall, 2000, p. 10.
20. Quoted in Ray. *African Religions*, p. 11.
21. Quoted in Ray. *African Religions*, p. 11.
22. Ray. *African Religions*, p. 12.

Chapter 3: Animal Tricksters

23. Quoted in Ray. *African Religions*, p. 16.
24. Quoted in Ray. *African Religions*, p. 16.
25. Quoted in Patricia Ann Lynch. "Ijapa." Facts On File History Database, June 22, 2014. www.fofweb .com/History/MainPrintPage.asp ?iPin=AMAZ118&DataType=Anc ient&WinType=Free.
26. Quoted in Melville J. Herskovits and Frances S. Herskovits. *An Outline of Dahomean Religious Belief*. Menasha, WI: American Anthropological Association, 1933, p. 56.
27. Quoted in Herskovits and Herskovits. *An Outline of Dahomean Religious Belief*, p. 37.
28. Ralph Ellison. *Invisible Man*. New York: Vintage, 1952, p. 16.

Chapter 4: Spirits, Magic, and Ceremonies

29. E. Bolaji Idowu. *African Traditional Religion*. Maryknoll, NY: Orbis, 1973, p. 177.
30. Idowu. *African Traditional Religion*, p. 177.
31. Elizabeth McAlister. "Praying for the Worst." *Los Angeles Times*, June 25, 2014, p. A13.
32. Quoted in Barnes and Ben-Amos. *Africa's Ogun, Old World and New*, p. 207.
33. David Cumes. "South African Indigenous Healing: How It Works." *Explore*, January 2013. www.explorejournal.com/article /S1550-8307(12)00225-X/fulltext #sec1.
34. Cumes. "South African Indigenous Healing."
35. Cumes. "South African Indigenous Healing."

Chapter 5: Ancient Beliefs in the New World

36. Ford. *The Hero with an African Face*, p. 6.
37. Quoted in Alfred Métraux. *Voodoo in Haiti*. New York: Schocken, 1972, p. 33.
38. Quoted in Leslie G. Desmangles. *The Faces of the Gods*. Chapel Hill: University of North Carolina Press, 1992, p. 109.
39. Quoted in Roy Rosenzweig Center for History and New Media. "Voodoo," 2014. https://chnm.gmu.edu /revolution/d/336/.
40. Cynthia Duncan. "Communication with the Orichás Through Music." About Santeria, January 19, 2014. www.aboutsanteria.com/protocol -for-drumming-ceremonies.html.

41. Cynthia Duncan. "Trance Possession." About Santeria, January 19, 2014. www.aboutsanteria.com/trance-possession.html.
42. Duncan. "Trance Possession."
43. Cynthia Duncan. "What Is Aché?" About Santeria, January 19, 2014. www.aboutsanteria.com/acheacute.html.
44. Joseph M. Murphy. *Santeria*. Boston: Beacon, 1993, p. 41.
45. Murphy. *Santeria*, p. 44.

animism: The idea that nonhuman entities such as animals and plants, objects such as mountains, and phenomena such as lightning possess animated spiritual essences.

babalow: The father of secrets, or diviner who interprets the patterns of the palm nuts when practicing Ifa, the Yoruba system of foretelling future events.

cardinal points: The four directions of north, south, east, and west, represented in mythology as earth, fire, air, and water, respectively.

cult: Latin for "care," cults in ancient Africa were religious groups that offered prayers and sacrifices for and built shrines to a specific deity or group of deities.

divination: The art of fortune telling or predicting the future.

orisha: The term used to describe the numerous gods, goddesses, and nature spirits in the Yoruba pantheon.

pantheon: All the gods and goddesses of a particular people considered as a group.

papyrus: A thin paper made from the reed-like papyrus plant.

relief: Sculptures with raised or sunken figures carved into flat panels of stone, wood, or other material.

smelting: The process of using heat and chemicals to produce iron or other metals.

trickster: A god who uses disguises, deception, and trickery to spread confusion and conflict and ruin people's plans.

Books

Tony Allan, Fergus Fleming, and Charles Phillips. *African Myths and Beliefs*. New York: Rosen, 2011. This book explores the myths and legends of sub-Saharan Africa.

Douglas C. Fox and Leo Frobenius. *African Genesis: Folk Tales and Myths of Africa*. Mineola, NY: Rosen, 2011. This book contains dozens of entertaining tales based on African mythology, including creation legends, trickster myths, and animal stories.

Patricia Ann Lynch. *African Mythology A–Z*. New York: Chelsea House, 2010. This book provides a comprehensive examination of the deities, places, events, animals, and beliefs that appear in the complex myths of the African people.

Kemba Mchawi. *Growing Up Yoruba: A Teen Guide Book for Practicing the Yoruba Lucumi Tradition*. Atlanta: WaterHears, 2013. A guide offering insight into Santeria and its relationship to ancient Yoruba practices, aimed at young adults who wish to learn more about the religion.

P. James Oliver. *Mansa Musa and the Empire of Mali*. Seattle: CreateSpace, 2013. A well-researched biography of Mansa Musa, Mali's emperor during its fourteenth-century golden age.

Websites

About Santeria (www.aboutsanteria .com). Created by a Santeria priestess, this website provides extensive knowledge about the religion, including history, spiritual practices, photos, and descriptions and illustrations of deities, or orishas.

African Mythology (www.godchecker .com/pantheon/african-mythology .php). This site features the mythology of Yoruba spirits such as Eleguá, Eshu, Obatala, and others.

A-Gallery (www.a-gallery.de). A web gallery of contemporary paintings by East and South African artists, with links to pages featuring extensive coverage of African myths, legends, beliefs, and folktales. Readers can discover the roles of trees, elephants, sunbirds, and the afterlife in African mythology.

Erzulies (http://erzulies.com/about-haitian-vodou-haitian-voodoo-history-beliefs). This site, hosted by a New Orleans voodoo store, explains Haitian voodoo practices and history, explores the Rada and Petro pantheons, and describes the initiation process and code of conduct for the religion.

***Myths and Legends of the Bantu,* Internet Sacred Text Archive** (www.sacred-texts.com/afr/mlb). This Internet copy of the 1933 book by the respected writer and Bantu-language teacher Alice Werner provides a comprehensive look at Bantu mythology, including creation myths, trickster tales, and stories of animal gods.

INDEX

PICTURE CREDITS

Cover: © Terry W. Ryder/Shutterstock
.com
© AFP/Getty Images, 70
© Art Directors & TRIP/Alamy, 28
© Benedicte Desrus/Alamy, 91
© Caroline Penn/Alamy, 82
© De Agostino Picture Library/Getty
Images, 25, 47
© Eric Nathan/Alamy, 65
© Gale/Cengage, 4, 5, 6
© Getty Images, 35
© Hemis/Alamy, 67
© Heritage Image Partnership Ltd/
Alamy, 15, 20, 32, 33, 52, 72
© HIP/Art Resource, NY, 31, 39
© Ivan Vdovin/Alamy, 51
© Jason Rothe/Alamy, 87
© Jim West/Alamy, 89

© Leon Swart/Alamy, 49
© Louise Batalla Duran/Alamy, 81
© Mary Evans Picture Library/Alamy,
9
© MJ Photography/Alamy, 14
© Niday Picture Library/Alamy, 76
© North Wind Picture Archives/Alamy,
41
© Old Papers Studio/Alamy, 45
© Oldtime/Alamy, 17
© Peter Horree/Alamy, 60
© Premaphotos/Alamy, 55
© Robert Brook/Alamy, 85
© Sally Mundy/Alamy, 78
© SSPL via Getty Images, 66
© UIG via Getty Images, 23
© Walt Disney/The Kobal Collection,
57

ABOUT THE AUTHOR

Stuart A. Kallen is the author of more than three hundred nonfiction books for children and young adults. He has written extensively about science, the environment, music, history, and mythology. In addition, Kallen has written award-winning children's videos and television scripts. In his spare time he sings, writes songs, and plays the guitar. Kallen lives in San Diego, California.